"Charles Billingsley has been leading people into a deeper sense of devotion and a lifestyle of worship. Now, you can be encouraged daily by the Word and by Charles through this daily devotional."

Ed Stetzer, Billy Graham Distinguished Chair,
Wheaton College

"When our lifestyle is full of worship, then our lives are full of meaning. That's why I'm so grateful for Charles's new devotional—he helps us do just that, live worshipfully!"

Jennifer Rothschild, author of *Lessons I Learned in the Dark*
and *66 Ways God Loves You*

"A lifestyle of worship is so much more than singing a song to the Lord. It's giving God glory in the way we live, love, and serve. To know Charles is to see a person who truly loves God with all of his heart and it spills out into every aspect of his life."

Denise Jones, Point of Grace

"For years, I have been inspired by Charles Billingsley's music. Thanks to his poignant book, *Words on Worship*, I am blessed by his encouraging words. He inspires me to be a more devoted disciple of Christ."

Babbie Mason, award-winning singer,
songwriter, and author

"Charles Billingsley ranks among the best worship leaders of this generation. The words he writes will awaken your heart to pursue worship as a lifestyle."

Margaret Feinberg, author of *Flourish*
and *Fight Back With Joy*

"Charles Billingsley brings excellence in worship. But more important than that, he brings authenticity, a heart, and message that goes beyond a song."

Anthony Evans, president/CEO, Anthony Evans Entertainment/
Sherman James Productions

"I love Charles. He is a leader among worship leaders. This devotional will be of great value to me and many other worship pastors."

Clay Crosse, worship leader and concert artist

"Charles's greatest gift is not his amazing vocal ability, but his ability to lead people to the throne of God in true, God-honoring worship."

Tony Perkins, president, Family Research Council

"*Words on Worship* is a must have. Charles has created a vital and useful tool to help us all continually fix our gaze on the only one who satisfies and the only one worthy of our total worship, Jesus."

Michael Neale, singer/songwriter and worship pastor
Prestonwood Baptist Church, Plano, Texas

"Charles Billingsley gives us a great gift—moments of quiet in an ever chaotic world."

Johnnie Moore, bestselling author, founder and CEO
of The KAIROS Company

"I am always in search of a devotional book that has immediacy and life application. Pastor Billingsley's latest book does just that!"

Buzz Williams, head basketball coach, Virginia Tech

Words on Worship

DEVOTIONS OF PRAISE

CHARLES BILLINGSLEY

WORTHY®
Inspired

Published by Worthy Inspired, an imprint of Worthy Publishing Group, a division of Worthy Media, Inc., One Franklin Park, 6100 Tower Circle, Suite 210, Franklin, TN 37067.

WORTHY is a registered trademark of Worthy Media, Inc.

HELPING PEOPLE EXPERIENCE THE HEART OF GOD

Library of Congress Cataloging-in-Publication Data

Names: Billingsley, Charles, author.
Title: Words on worship : devotions of praise / by Charles Billingsley.
Description: Franklin, TN : Worthy Publishing, 2016.
Identifiers: LCCN 2016045248 | ISBN 9781617958489 (hardcover)
Subjects: LCSH: Devotional literature. | Worship.
Classification: LCC BV4832.3 .B54 2016 | DDC 248.3--dc23
LC record available at https://lccn.loc.gov/2016045248

ISBN: 978-1-61795-848-9

For foreign and subsidiary rights, contact rights@worthypublishing.com

Cover Design: Marc Whitaker

Printed in the United States of America

17 18 19 20 21 LBM 10 9 8 7 6 5 4 3 2 1

FOREWORD
BY DR. DAVID JEREMIAH

For more than fifteen years I have been watching Charles Billingsley lead worship. I continue to be amazed at his ability to motivate people from every age and stage of life to lift their voices in praise to the Lord.

When I heard that Charles was going to put some of his thoughts about worship into print, I wanted to add my name to the project.

Charles Billingsley lights up when he talks about worship, especially when the worshippers connect with the Lord and with each other.

In his writing you will discover why he has devoted his life to teaching and to modeling this calling he has upon his life.

Recorded versions of his essays on worship can be heard five days a week on more than three hundred radio stations across the United States.

As you read these short entries, I predict that you will be led in a whole new way to worship God with "all that is within [you]" (Psalm 103:1).

Happy are those who hear
the joyful call to worship,
for they will walk in the light
of your presence, LORD.

PSALM 89:15

The Most Important Thing You Can Do

What does the LORD your God require of you? He requires only that you fear the LORD your God, and live in a way that pleases him, and love him and serve him with all your heart and soul. And you must always obey the LORD's commands and decrees that I am giving you today for your own good.

DEUTERONOMY 10:12–13

What is the most important thing you can do in your life? That's a big question! If I were to stand on a busy street corner and poll a thousand people, I would probably get a thousand different answers.

Jesus was asked this same question by a religious leader of His day, except the question was phrased like this: "Of all the commandments, which is the most important?" To which Jesus replied: "Love the Lord your God with all your heart, all your soul, all your mind, and with all your strength" (Mark 12:28, 30).

Do you know what worship is? It is that right there: to love the Lord with all your heart, soul, mind, and strength. As you move throughout your day, remember that the most important thing you can do in your life is to simply love God. All He wants is all of you.

Lord, thank You that what you require of me is simply that I love You and follow You with all of my being. Help me today to live for You.

Do You Recognize the Voice of God?

My sheep listen to my voice; I know them, and they follow me.

JOHN 10:27

We live in a noisy world. Moments of absolute silence are rare. In fact, some of us actually sleep better with a noisemaker. We have grown so accustomed to noise that total silence is eerie and makes us uncomfortable. But have you ever considered that the word *listen* contains the same letters as the word *silent*?

One of the best ways we can worship Him today is to get alone, turn the noise off, and rest in the silence. Psalm 46:10 puts it this way: "Be still, and know that I am God!" It is in the stillness that we hear and recognize His voice.

When life gets stressful, focus on God. In Isaiah 26:3 we're reminded, "You will keep in perfect peace all who trust in you, all whose thoughts are fixed on you!" Stress is predictable. So when it hits, find peace and comfort and rest in the Lord. Worship Him in the midst of it all and you'll find that He helps you through it all. Listen for His still, small voice in your heart today whispering words of peace.

Father, You're so good to remind me to be still before You. Help me to quiet the noise and shut out the distractions that I might rest in Your presence awhile.

Will You Worship God with Open Hands?

I will praise you as long as I live, lifting up my hands to you in prayer.

PSALM 63:4

Hands speak a language of their own, don't they? Hands held up can mean praise or even surrender. Hands held out with palms up can mean either I'm giving something to you or you're giving something to me. Closed hands can be a sign of aggression as they form a fist. You get the idea.

As we approach worship, I encourage you to live with open hands. It is only with open hands that we can give something away, but it's also only with open hands that we can receive.

Worship always includes three elements: glory, dedication, and sacrifice. Lifting our hands in praise is ascribing glory to God, but reaching out our hands in service requires sacrifice. Both acts serve a proper purpose in worship, and our walk with God requires both.

Worship is you and me giving our hearts in praise to God, but He is gracious in that He blesses us in return for our praise. The God who has given so much still wants to give us more. Isn't that just like Him? So worship the Lord with open hands, ready to give, ready to serve. You never know what blessings God will put back into those open hands of yours.

Here are my hands, Lord—open, available. Whom would You have me reach out to today with Your love?

Salty Worshipers

Once you were full of darkness, but now you have light from the Lord. So live as people of light! For this light within you produces only what is good and right and true. Carefully determine what pleases the Lord.

EPHESIANS 5:8—10

Salt has many valuable uses. It preserves, it flavors, and it purifies. Jesus must have had that in mind when He told us, "You are the salt of the earth; but if the salt loses its flavor, how shall it be seasoned? It is then good for nothing but to be thrown out and trampled underfoot by men" (Matthew 5:13 NKJV).

As the salt of the earth, it is our job to do all we can to preserve the moral fiber of our nation and hinder the spread of corruption. We accomplish this by wising up to the mentality of our culture—by learning why people believe what they believe—so we can discover how to bring change to our world through the power of His Spirit and the truth of His Word. We cannot afford to sit idly by and watch a generation grow up around us who have never been exposed to true worshipers. We must learn how to combat the sin of our time while at the same time truly love the sinner with the compassion of Christ. Not an easy balance to find, but necessary.

Know what you believe and why you believe it, and then stand strong and steady as the salt of the earth.

Jesus, show me what it looks like to be salt in my corner of the world!

Beware of the Pharisee

God saved you by his grace when you believed. And you can't take credit for this; it is a gift from God. Salvation is not a reward for the good things we have done, so none of us can boast about it. For we are God's masterpiece.

EPHESIANS 2:8–10

If you've been a Christian long, you know we all have a tendency to become pharisaical at times. Depending on our background and denominational upbringing, we all have certain so-called sins that we consider worse than others, even if we don't publicly admit it.

Pharisees in the days of Jesus were the church crowd, but not the loving, grace-giving church crowd. These guys were a religious sect obsessed with following the law to the last detail. They were harsh and judgmental to those who didn't. They were religious for all the wrong reasons. For the Pharisee, life wasn't about having a loving, thriving relationship with God. Rules trumped relationship.

You know, society is still doing that today, even among churchgoers. As a follower and worshiper of Jesus, I challenge you today to raise the standard of living in your world by shedding any legalistic mind-set you might have. Embrace the grace-giving love of Jesus. Live your faith with an authentic love for Jesus. Let His grace shine through you because of your faith in Him.

Lord, may my life be a reflection of the grace You have so abundantly bestowed on me.

Worship God with a Clean Heart

Create in me a clean heart, O God. Renew a loyal spirit within me.

PSALM 51:10

My little boy once asked me, "Do I have to use soap *every* time I take a shower?" Of course my answer was yes! The water of a shower does wonders, but it's the soap that washes the dirt away thoroughly. And just as soap gets the dirt off our skin, so the blood of Jesus cleanses us from our sin. We read in 1 John 1:9, "If we confess our sins, He is faithful and just to forgive us our sins and to cleanse us from all unrighteousness" (NKJV).

Everyone sins; that's just a fact. But when we sin, we must repent and turn from it so it doesn't become a habit or a practice in our lives. When we don't confess our sin, our fellowship with God is weakened, and our worship becomes distant and strained. To repent means to make an about-face, to turn from the way we were heading and go the opposite direction. As worshipers, we must regularly confess our sins and work to stay in right relationship with the Lord.

So, next time you shower and reach for the soap, be reminded of the cleansing power of Jesus's blood. Because He died on the cross for you and me, we can worship Him with a clean heart and a pure life.

Father, thank You for being faithful and just to forgive. Help me to be quick to repent when I sin!

Make Jesus the Focus of Your Worship

Christ is also the head of the church, which is his body. He is the beginning, supreme over all who rise from the dead. So he is first in everything.

COLOSSIANS 1:18

Jesus should always be the object of our worship. Philippians 2:10 reminds us that one day every knee will bow and every tongue confess the name of Jesus. Every living being—angels and humans alike—will bow before King Jesus, the Author and Finisher of our faith. It is only Jesus who has the right of sovereignty, "for in him all things were created. . . . He is before all things and in him all things hold together" (1:16–17 NIV).

So let me ask you this: Is worshiping Jesus a regular practice in your life? It should be the most natural thing for us as Christians to place Jesus in a position of preeminence in our lives. But many times—maybe not in belief, but in action—we relegate Him to just another religious object to be brought out for a Sunday morning experience.

Remember today that Jesus is the very image of the invisible Creator God. He is God in the flesh, the One for whom all things were created. Worship Him today as King of kings and Lord of lords and let His majesty consume your lifestyle of worship.

Jesus, it's all about You! Reign in me today. Help me to keep You in the place of preeminence in my life.

Worship the Lord by Seeking His Face

When You said, "Seek My face," my heart said to You, "Your face, LORD, I will seek."

PSALM 27:8 NKJV

Second Chronicles 7:14 gives us a four-step process for personal revival. In this verse the Lord tells us we are to humble ourselves, pray, seek His face, and turn from our sin. I love the phrase "seek His face." It implies we are to seek the very heart and mind of God. We are to seek after who He is.

Too often we seek the hand of God before we seek the face of God. When we seek God's hand, we are looking for what God can do. When we seek the face of God, we are looking at who God is. Although it is perfectly natural for us as His children to seek both the hand and face of God, many times we seek His hand first in order to bring us an experience or deliver us out of trouble. He is certainly capable and willing, but to seek His face means we come to Him seeking His agenda instead of our own.

So if you want revival in your life of worship, begin by humbling yourself, praying, and earnestly seeking the face of God, not just His hand.

O God, I bow before You now in adoration and worship. Have Your way in my life today!

Learn to Practice the Wisdom of Firsts

"Bring all the tithes into the storehouse so there will be enough food in my Temple. If you do," says the LORD of Heaven's Armies, "I will open the windows of heaven for you. I will pour out a blessing so great you won't have enough room to take it in! Try it! Put me to the test!"

MALACHI 3:10

When I was in college, a wise professor told me to start practicing the wisdom of firsts. By that he meant that I should make it a habit of giving God the first part of everything in my life. That way, I ensure that God is getting the best part of me rather than the leftovers.

The formula is simple: Give God the first of everything in my life. At minimum, the first tenth of every dollar should go to God. The first moments of every day should be reserved for time alone with God. The first one I should go to when I am in need is God. The first day of the week should be set aside to honor the Lord and fellowship with His people in church. And on and on the list goes. I think you get the idea.

I encourage you today to give God your very best. Practice the wisdom of worshiping God with your firsts and then watch how He blesses your life!

Lord, all I have belongs to You. What changes do I need to make to ensure I'm giving You the first of everything in my life?

What Does Real Love Look Like?

We love each other because he loved us first.

1 JOHN 4:19

In a day and age when the word *love* is flippantly thrown about in reference to anything from football to food and family, it's sometimes hard to gain a clear understanding of what real love looks like. So what does it look like? Well, it's like Saint Augustine said: "Love has the hands to help others. It has the feet to hasten to the poor and needy. It has eyes to see misery and want. It has the ears to hear the sighs and sorrows of men. That is what love looks like."

The Bible reminds us in 1 John that "God is love." True love in its purest form comes only from God. What we need to understand is that you and I would have no capacity to love others if God had not loved us first. It is His love for us that gives us a reason for hope today. It was His sacrifice that brings us His reward. He loves us so much that He made the ultimate sacrifice for us. Because God so loved the world, He gave us His Son, Jesus, the embodiment of love.

So, what does love look like? Jesus! Let Jesus be your example of how to truly love others.

May I be so filled with the awareness of Your love for me, Jesus, that it can't help but overflow to everyone around me!

What Is the Purpose of Worship?

You must serve only the LORD your God. If you do, I will bless you with food and water, and I will protect you from illness.

EXODUS 23:25

We all worship something or someone. I believe it's safe to say we worship that which we live for. And we live for that which we worship. We are created beings and have a natural inclination, a built-in desire, to worship something or someone. The problem is, many of us end up worshiping a creation of some sort rather than the Creator Himself. But the purpose of worship is so that you and I can fulfill our purpose in life. We were created to worship God. We were made to live for Him and enjoy Him forever.

If you are not living a lifestyle of worship, then you are missing the whole purpose of your existence. I realize that may sound like a broad and far-fetched statement, but it really is the truth. The beautiful thing is, even though God should be the object of our worship, somehow He takes our worship and turns it into a blessing for us. So the purpose of our worship is to honor and bless the Lord, but the result of worship is that He, in turn, blesses us. Isn't that just like God?

Worship the Giver of life today with all that you are.

Glorious God, You are worthy of all worship and praise!

Undivided Worship

Come, let us worship and bow down. Let us kneel before the Lord our maker.

PSALM 95:6

It's a common practice for churches to have multiple styles of worship services. Of course, when we say "style" it almost always refers to the music. Unfortunately, in our efforts to please everyone, church leaders are prone to cater to the preferences of the people rather than leading by vision. We must understand that worship services in our local church body should not be planned around our personal preferences. Rather, our worship services should be focused on dwelling in God's presence. It is only in the manifest presence of God that we will truly see lives changed and hearts tuned in to worshiping in spirit and in truth.

Worship also requires preparation on our part, personally and corporately. Personal worship prepares us for corporate worship, and corporate worship prepares us for personal worship. In other words, the time we spend with Jesus during the week will have a direct impact on how we respond to His presence on Sunday morning at church. Worship happens when our hearts are prepared to be in His presence.

So remember, worship is not a style and it's not a song. Worship in our churches happens when one godly believer joins the company of other believers to celebrate the presence of God regardless of the style of the music.

Lord, when I gather with other believers in Your house, help us to put our differences aside and simply celebrate Your presence.

You Are the Light of the World

You are the light of the world. . . . Let your good deeds shine out for all to see, so that everyone will praise your heavenly Father.

MATTHEW 5:14, 16

There are many mornings when I awake much earlier than the rest of my household. In those early mornings, when it's still dark, to avoid waking my wife I quickly turn on the bathroom light and then close the door so I can see just enough light through the crack at the bottom of the door to get dressed in the closet. Believe it or not, in a dark house, that little bit of light goes a long way.

You know, Jesus said that as His children, we are the "light of the world." He gave us this word more as a statement than a command. In other words, as followers of Him, we become a reflection of His glory. It is simply our reality. He is Light. We are His reflection.

You may work in a dark place or even live in a dark home, but the Light of Christ can shine through you brightly. That's what worshipers are: shining lights of praise that bring glory to God and point others to the light of His love. Let your light shine in all you do, even the little things.

May I be a reflection of Your light today, Jesus, in a dark world that desperately needs You.

All He Wants Is All of You

The earth is the LORD's, and everything in it. The world and all its people belong to him.

PSALM 24:1

God owns everything. If we were to ask God in an interview what the size of His portfolio is, He would say, "All of it." God owns it all. Not only that, God is over it all and created it all! In Isaiah 44:24 God reminds us: "I am the LORD, who makes all things, who stretches out the heavens all alone, who spreads abroad the earth by Myself" (NKJV).

Isn't it comforting to know that the God we worship owns and holds absolutely everything in His hands, including you—and your portfolio? We must get it into our minds that our money is God's money. Every financial decision we make is a spiritual decision, because it's not our money to begin with. We are simply managing what He owns. He has given us everything and He owns everything. When we surrender our lives to Him as His servants, we give everything back to Him. We are simply stewards now of all the blessings we possess.

I challenge you today to worship God by placing your money and your life solely into His hands. He is Lord over all, so all He wants is all of you.

Heavenly Father, thank You for the many material blessings You've bestowed on me. May I be ever mindful that all I have belongs to You and live accordingly.

Worship the God of Order

May the Lord of peace himself give you his peace at all times and in every situation. The Lord be with you all.

2 THESSALONIANS 3:16

Has it ever occurred to you that nothing ever occurs to God? The God we worship doesn't operate out of chaos. He doesn't make His decisions on a whim, nor does He live reactively. He is sovereign. He is in control. Omniscient, omnipotent, and omnipresent. He is all-seeing, all-powerful, and all-present. God has an order and a plan and nothing catches Him by surprise. Doesn't that ease your mind? To think that in this crazy, chaotic world, God is still on the throne and still firmly in control?

I know sometimes it doesn't feel like it, but you can rest assured that the One who formed the earth and the heavens with His fingers has a firm grasp of all that is happening in your world. First Corinthians 14:33 reminds us that "God is not the author of confusion but of peace" (NKJV). As worshipers of God, we are always in His presence. He is not far away, dear friend. He is right beside you, and you are under the shadow of the Almighty. So the next time you feel a little antsy about your future, remember that you are held firmly in the hands of our all-powerful, all-knowing God.

Faithful Father, I'm grateful that You are in control; nothing that happens in my life takes You by surprise. Nothing can touch me without Your permission.

Worship as a Peacemaker

Those who are peacemakers will plant seeds of peace and reap a harvest of righteousness.

JAMES 3:18

God is a God of peace. Jesus came that we might have peace, and ultimately that there would be peace in this world. However, our understanding of peace and the world's understanding of peace are two different things. True peace begins and ends with peace in the heart of the individual. Being at peace about the condition of your soul allows you to live at peace with others.

When I picture peace, I imagine a lighthouse in the midst of a crazy storm. Waves are tossing a ship to and fro as the captain desperately seeks the safety of shore. Then suddenly, he sees the lighthouse, a symbol of stability and safety and peace. This is a picture of how each believer should be around those who do not know the Lord. This kind of peace brings a supernatural calm amid the noise of a chaotic world, and stability and harmony to a divided culture.

"Blessed are the peacemakers," Jesus said, "for they shall be called sons of God" (Matthew 5:9 NKJV). True peacemakers are those who promote the love of God and the kingdom of God. All worshipers of Jesus should relentlessly pursue peace in conflict and calm in chaos. Will you be a peacemaker today?

Help me today, Jesus, to be a peacemaker in my corner of the world.

Worship with Familiar Faith

The eyes of the LORD search the whole earth in order to strengthen those whose hearts are fully committed to him.

2 CHRONICLES 16:9

We live every day by faith in things we don't understand or haven't even experienced. For instance, when you visit the doctor, you sit in a chair in the waiting room that you've probably never sat in before. By faith you believe that chair will hold you up. By faith you drive down the road trusting that people you've never met will stay on their side of the road and not hit you.

We live by faith in the little things of life all the time because these things are familiar. So why is it so hard to live by faith when it comes to the big decisions of life? I sincerely believe it's because we haven't gotten familiar with what it's like to rely on God on a daily basis. We don't know Him as we should.

I challenge you to exercise your faith today by drawing closer to Jesus. Ask God to give you a broader glimpse of who He is, of how trustworthy He is. Bring your needs and concerns to Him. Tune your heart to His voice. When His voice is familiar, it is easier to trust Him.

Lord, remind me today how trustworthy You are. Thank You that I can trust You with the big things in my life as well as the little things. Help me tune my ears to hear Your voice!

The Indestructible Blessings of God

I give them eternal life, and they will never perish. No one can snatch them away from me, for my Father has given them to me, and he is more powerful than anyone else. No one can snatch them from the Father's hand.

JOHN 10:28–29

One of the most comforting things about being a Christian is the security it gives our souls, both now and forever. The apostle Peter reminded us of this security when he wrote, "Blessed be the God and Father of our Lord Jesus Christ, who according to His abundant mercy has begotten us again to a living hope through the resurrection of Jesus Christ from the dead, to an inheritance incorruptible and undefiled and that does *not* fade away, reserved in heaven for you, who are *kept* by the power of God through faith for salvation ready to be revealed in the last time" (1 Peter 1:3–5 NKJV, emphasis added).

The word *kept* in the Greek literally means "to be garrisoned by an army." Fellow believer, you are not only held in the eternal arms of the Lord now, you are kept and protected forever. Your soul is eternally secure. You can rest in the hands of the Almighty. He will not let you go, and His Word promises that nothing can pluck you out of His hands. So live with confidence today and worship Him as a lifestyle.

Thank You, heavenly Father, for the security and safety that are mine in You!

Worship with a Healthy Self-Image

You must have the same attitude that Christ Jesus had. Though he was God, he did not think of equality with God as something to cling to. Instead, he gave up his divine privileges; he took the humble position of a slave and was born as a human being. When he appeared in human form, he humbled himself in obedience to God and died a criminal's death on a cross.

PHILIPPIANS 2:5–8

Philippians 2:5–11 is one of my favorite passages in the Bible. Paul begins these verses by reminding us of the decision Jesus made to leave His throne in heaven, renounce the privileges of deity, and dress down in human flesh in order to become a humble servant. If ever there was a model for humility, Jesus is it.

As we strive toward a lifestyle of worship, we would do well to imitate Him as much as possible. Obviously we don't have a throne in heaven, but each one of us is in a position of influence over someone. Now, humility is not a spirit of self-deprecation or self-loathing. Rather, it is having a healthy understanding of our strengths and weaknesses, and then being honest about both and no longer feeling the need to impress everybody all the time. This self-confidence comes from our unwavering faith in the Lord Jesus. That alone gives us the ability to relate well with others. Let's humble ourselves in the sight of God today and worship Him in humility.

Help me today, Lord, to follow Your example of humility.

How Do I Love God with All of My Heart?

"This is the way to have eternal life—to know you, the only true God, and Jesus Christ, the one you sent to earth."

JOHN 17:3

Have you ever loved someone so much that thoughts of them consumed you? Some of you may be that in love right now, and just reading these words is causing you to get distracted with thoughts of that person. Why do you love that person? Because you *know* that person. And because you know that special someone so well, he or she has captured your heart. You find you want to spend every moment with him or her.

According to Jesus, the greatest commandment of all is to love God with our whole heart. That is the single most important thing we can do. In fact, it is the very reason we exist. But we will never truly love God until we know God.

Do you know God? Do you know how much He loves you? How, you may ask, do I get to know God? Spend time in His presence. Talk with Him throughout your day, read His Word, ask Him to reveal Himself to you and show you how much He loves you. You will find that to know Him is to love Him.

Jesus, I want to know You and fall more deeply in love with You. Please reveal Yourself to me!

How Do I Love God with All of My Soul?

O God, you are my God; I earnestly search for you. My soul thirsts for you; my whole body longs for you in this parched and weary land where there is no water.

PSALM 63:1

In the previous entry we talked about loving God with our whole heart, so today let's talk about loving God with our soul. Our souls are the deepest part of our nature. It is the part of us that stays alive after our bodies are dead. You can kill the body, but you can't kill the soul. The soul is eternal. Incidentally, the only thing we do here on this earth that we will also do in heaven is worship our Savior.

Deep within every human soul there is a God-shaped void that each of us desperately tries to fill. The trouble is, we are too quick to chase after worthless things that can't fill the emptiness. God is the only one who can satisfy the soul and give it meaning and purpose.

To love God with all our soul is to worship Him from the innermost part of our being, the part of us that lasts forever. David said in Psalm 63, "My soul thirsts for God." Can we say the same today?

God, too often I chase after earthly things to fill the emptiness in my soul but only You can satisfy. Help me to be able to truthfully say that my soul thirsts for You.

How Do I Love God with All of My Mind?

We are instructed to turn from godless living and sinful pleasures. We should live in this evil world with wisdom, righteousness, and devotion to God.

TITUS 2:12

To love God with all of our mind is a difficult thing to do because our lives are so full of distractions. In fact, the average person has over seventy thousand thoughts a day! If you feel like you have a hard time staying focused, you aren't the only one.

So how can we love God with all our mind? It begins with three key ingredients: vision, discipline, and accomplishment. Vision is the ability to see in your mind's eye where you want to be. Discipline is the bridge you must cross on a daily basis in order to reach that accomplishment. Both vision and discipline start in the mind. So if our minds are cluttered with all kinds of images and thoughts that distract us from our vision, we will never accomplish what we set out to do.

All of this applies to growing spiritually. Worship starts with the mind, then becomes a response of the heart. Growing closer to Jesus takes work. It takes time and it takes discipline. Remember the words of Jesus, "If any of you wants to be my follower, you must give up your own way, take up your cross daily, and follow me" (Luke 9:23).

I pray for Your grace, Lord, to discipline my mind that You might be glorified.

How Do I Worship God with All My Will?

All athletes are disciplined in their training. They do it to win a prize that will fade away, but we do it for an eternal prize.

1 CORINTHIANS 9:25

When an athlete is striving to win a championship, he cannot do so without that special intangible attribute called the will. He must have the will to win, or he will lose. He has to have that certain "want to" that comes from deep within his heart, or a championship is almost impossible to achieve. Many have referred to this "will" as having the "heart of a champion."

It is with this same mind-set that we should approach worshiping the Lord each day. Jesus said the greatest commandment of all is to worship the Lord with all our heart, soul, mind, and strength. I would encourage you to approach your worship of God today as an athlete would: with a disciplined, determined, and diligent will. Make the choice to stay committed to the course. We must not only see the big picture of where we want to end up, but we must also have the intestinal fortitude to keep going even when it's not easy. There will be ups and downs and moments of adversity, but let's not forget, nothing of any value ever comes without a price.

Lord, I declare that in You I have the heart of a champion. I will stay the course and worship You with all that I am.

How Do I Worship God with My Body?

Don't you realize that your body is the temple of the Holy Spirit, who lives in you and was given to you by God? You do not belong to yourself, for God bought you with a high price. So you must honor God with your body.

I CORINTHIANS 6:19–20

Worshiping God with our bodies is quite different from worshiping the body itself. We live in a culture that is obsessed with the body. For many, having a great body is the ultimate in success. And it's big business, too, reaching an average revenue of 21.4 billion dollars a year.

There's certainly nothing wrong with living a healthy lifestyle and eating properly. In fact, we should do that, as our bodies are temples of the Lord and we need to treat them as such. However, worshiping God with our bodies as a "living sacrifice," as Paul puts it in Romans 12, means we present all we are as an offering to God. Worship isn't just something we think about, it is something we do—with our hands, feet, ears, and eyes. It means we glorify God wherever we are and with whatever we are doing.

Remember, worship is you and me loving the Lord in all aspects of life. So jump in and worship God with your whole heart and your body.

I present my body to You as a living sacrifice, Lord. I've been bought with a price and I am not my own.

The Power of Gentleness

Blessed are the meek, for they shall inherit the earth.

MATTHEW 5:5 NKJV

Recently I was at a church where I met the largest man I had ever seen. He was almost seven feet tall and had muscles bulging everywhere, even from his earlobes. He was absolutely huge. Yet when I talked to him and observed how he interacted with others, especially children, it was very clear that this man was deeply loved and respected. His pastor later referred to him as a "gentle giant."

I love that phrase. In two words it says, "This man could crush you with one blow from his forearm but has the power within to control his reactions and his strength." That's what gentleness is: the power to control your reactions to difficult people and situations. It's responding with meekness rather than might. Meekness and gentleness should never be confused with weakness. It takes great strength and great discipline to live gently.

Those who know the Lord and who live their lives in such a way as to display meekness—who exercise self-control when times get tough—will inherit the new earth that God is preparing for eternity. In the meantime, we could all use a little more meekness in our lives. Those who are gentle and meek are humble, tempered, steady, and strong. Just like Jesus.

Jesus, may I become more like You—gentle and meek, steady and strong.

The Joy of the Lord

The joy of the LORD is your strength!

NEHEMIAH 8:10

There is a difference between happiness and joy. Happiness is based on circumstances and is temporary. I wish we all had continual happiness, but it's simply not possible. Bad things happen. But joy is eternal. Joy is deeper. Joy comes from the comfort of knowing God is able. It's not a "pie in the sky" mentality. Rather, it's real, calming, and confident.

Joy originates from God Himself. It is one of the many benefits of being God's child. True joy is one of the top characteristics of a worshiper. It is based on attitude and confidence. It's having the right attitude about every situation we face, both the good and the bad. It's having the confidence that Jesus is always there and in control no matter what happens.

There are many things in life that try to steal away the joy in our hearts. The loss of a loved one, financial struggles, disease, and sin will all make their way into most of our lives at some point. But for the growing, worshiping child of God, there should be an inner joy that resonates through it all. So trust Jesus, and rest in the joy only He can give.

Thank You, Jesus, for the joy that is mine in Christ. When times are hard, I pray that nothing will be able to steal it away!

Worship Requires Sacrifice

*Let us offer through Jesus a continual sacrifice of praise to God,
proclaiming our allegiance to his name.*

HEBREWS 13:15

When I was growing up, my church used to sing a popular song called "We Bring the Sacrifice of Praise." But as a kid I never really considered what those words truly meant. Now I think I understand better.

A "sacrifice of praise" can come in a variety of different ways, most commonly from our lips as we give thanks to His name. But a sacrifice of praise can also come from our wallets as we give, or our time as we serve, or our talents as we use them for God.

Of course the easiest sacrifice we can give to God is praise from our mouth and heart. This is commanded by God and should come naturally to us as His children. But if you want to take your worship of Him to another level, then offer a sacrifice of praise to Him in ways that cost you something more. It's wonderfully fulfilling to sing loudly and raise your hands in a worship service, but it's also easy. However, it is much more sacrificial to open your wallet or to give your time in service to the poor and needy.

Consider today how much more powerful your personal time of worship will be when you are living a lifestyle of sacrificial praise.

Father, may I be quick to offer You my sacrifices of praise!

The Root Determines the Fruit

Christ will make his home in your hearts as you trust in him. Your roots will grow down into God's love and keep you strong.

EPHESIANS 3:17

There are over 23,000 types of trees, and every type has roots. The root system of a tree usually grows between two to four times the width of the tree, establishing a foundation for growth, and is fed by the water and minerals of the soil. The better the soil, the stronger the roots, the healthier the tree. You can't see the roots, but they determine the health of that tree.

And so it goes in our lifestyle of worship. Jesus warned us about seed thrown in stony areas where the soil is bad: "A farmer . . . scattered [seed] across his field. . . . Some seeds fell . . . on shallow soil with underlying rock. The seeds sprouted quickly because the soil was shallow. But the plants soon wilted under the hot sun, and since they didn't have deep roots, they died" (Matthew 13:3–6).

Root your life in good soil. In other words, ground yourself in the Word of God and surround yourself with strong believers. Doing so will help you grow strong spiritual roots, which will provide the foundation for a fruitful life of worship.

Father, I want my roots to grow down deep in You. Help me to cultivate friendships with other strong believers and ground myself in Your Word.

We Worship a Holy God

No one is holy like the LORD! There is no one besides you; there is no Rock like our God.

1 SAMUEL 2:2

God Almighty is the embodiment of holiness itself. Think of the most perfect thing you have ever seen. He is more perfect than that. His character is the very essence of righteousness, flawlessness, purity, and love. He has never had a thought that was wrong or a motive that was questionable. He was never created, He has always been. He is omnipotent, omniscient, and omnipresent. There is nothing He cannot see, nothing He cannot overcome, nothing He cannot do, nothing He has not created, and nothing He cannot defeat.

He is great and awesome, worthy, mighty, excellent, incredible, indescribable, and infallible, but do you know His most significant attribute of all? He is holy. Right now, and for all eternity, the angels in glory chant unceasingly: "Holy, holy, holy is the Lord God, the Almighty" (Revelation 4:8).

When we see God in His holiness, our weaknesses, failures, and sins are vividly exposed and we see ourselves for who we really are: helpless sinners in the hands of a holy God. And yet He loves us anyway. When we are able to finally grasp that great truth, our response is always worship from the bottom of our hearts. It is His holiness more than any other attribute that makes Him worthy of our praise.

My Redeemer and Savior, I praise You for Your holiness!

Without Love,
We Are Bankrupt

Since God chose you to be the holy people he loves, you must clothe yourselves with tenderhearted mercy, kindness, humility, gentleness, and patience.

COLOSSIANS 3:12

Have you ever considered the fact that you can be rich with money but still live a bankrupt life? The apostle Paul said as much in 1 Corinthians 13:3: "No matter what I say, what I believe, and what I do, I'm bankrupt without love" (MSG).

Every one of us has someone in our lives whom we love and who we know loves us. And each and every day we have the opportunity to make deposits into their lives. So go ahead and send them an encouraging note or text. Tell them how much they mean to you. Or better yet, show them with some act of kindness or service. Those little acts are the foundational building blocks that create a rich life and honor God. You could be the very blessing that someone needs. You could be the vessel God uses on this day and in this moment to bless someone's heart or even save a life. It may take an extra moment or two . . . but it is an expression of worship.

So don't go bankrupt. Worship the Lord today by investing in the lives of others.

Thank You, Father, for the loved ones You've put in my life. May I be quick to grab every opportunity to make love deposits in their lives.

Serving Others
Is an Act of Worship

Don't be selfish; don't try to impress others. Be humble, thinking of others as better than yourselves. Don't look out only for your own interests, but take an interest in others, too.

PHILIPPIANS 2:3–4

When Jesus was being tempted by Satan in the wilderness, He taught us an important lesson about worship. Satan had just offered Jesus all the kingdoms of the earth if He would bow down and worship him, but Jesus replied, "It is written, 'You shall *worship* the LORD your God, and Him only you shall *serve*'" (Matthew 4:10 NKJV, emphasis added). Notice that He linked worship and service in His response. Could it be that when we *serve* others we *worship* our God?

Many times we feel the temptation to build ourselves up in the eyes of friends, family, neighbors, or coworkers. I encourage you to resist that temptation. Mother Teresa observed, "At the end of life we will not be judged by how many diplomas we have received, how much money we have made, or how many great things we have done. We will be judged by 'I was hungry, and you gave me something to eat, I was naked and you clothed me. I was homeless, and you took me in.'"

Today, humbly serve others, and as a result, you'll worship the living God.

Father, I worship You. Help me to put others before myself today and snatch the opportunities You put in my path to be a humble servant.

Find Rest in Jesus

I have given rest to the weary and joy to the sorrowing.

JEREMIAH 31:25

Have you ever been so tired you couldn't even sleep? The stress of the day has worn you down so much that you can't wait to hit the sack, only to discover your mind is still churning. Or maybe you feel like your life is beginning to fray around the edges. Perhaps you need to rediscover what it means to rest in Jesus.

Find a moment in each day to simply rest in Jesus. The best time might be right in the middle of the most stressful time. Take an inventory of your life and all its activities. What is the cause of your unrest? For a worshiper, the only answer for any of it is proper alignment in your walk with Jesus. "Come to me," Jesus says, "All of you who are weary and carry heavy burdens, and I will give you rest. Take my yoke upon you. Let me teach you, because I am humble and gentle at heart, and you will find rest for your souls" (Matthew 11:28–29).

Go to God and ask Him to settle your spirit. Let Him give you rest for your weary soul. Let Him smooth out those frayed edges in your life. You will discover that your worship will take on a much deeper meaning.

Jesus, when I'm overcome by the demands of life and my soul is weary, thank You that I can run to You for rest!

Have You Had Your Workout Today?

Physical training is good, but training for godliness is much better, promising benefits in this life and in the life to come.

1 TIMOTHY 4:8

I believe in exercise. Not only does it make me feel better, but it sharpens my mind and provides great benefits over a lifetime, like controlling my weight, strengthening my bones and muscles, and reducing stress.

However, as good as exercise is for the body, there is another exercise that is even more important: exercising godliness. Paul reminds his young disciple in 1 Timothy that bodily exercise does have some profit but that exercising godliness is infinitely more profitable. Why? Because godly living, or worshipful living, directly impacts every aspect of your life: the body, mind, and soul.

So even though exercising our bodies has some benefits on this earth, exercising godliness has unending benefits both now and for eternity. I encourage you to jump into the daily exercise of training for godliness. Start by pouring your heart out to God in prayer, seeking His help. Read the Word of God and take it to heart. This is the best kind of workout: a worship workout for the soul.

Father, I confess I have a lot of room to grow in this area! Show me not only how important it is to You that I be in training for godliness, but what that should look like in my life.

Are You Willing to Die for Your Faith?

God blesses those who are persecuted for doing right, for the Kingdom of Heaven is theirs.

MATTHEW 5:10

We live in a day when more Christians are being persecuted worldwide than at any other time in history. Last year alone over 200,000 Christians were martyred for their faith. These precious souls, like millions before them, paid the ultimate sacrifice in the name of our Savior. They should inspire us with their commitment to Jesus and willingness to suffer simply because they believed.

When we live boldly for Christ and display our faith publicly, people will clearly see it. Your neighbors, coworkers, friends, and family will have no doubt as to where your heart is. It doesn't mean we are obnoxious or rude or arrogant. Rather, they will know us by our love. And yet many will still be angered, and you will run the risk of persecution. Don't let any of this surprise you. Jesus warned us it would happen. Just remember the words of Christ: When you are persecuted for His name's sake, you will reap a great reward in heaven. And we will be in heaven far longer than we will be on this earth. Worship Him boldly today, and remember to pray for your brothers and sisters who are being persecuted for their faith.

Lord, may I live boldly for You, unafraid to tell others about You and live my life for You!

Enduring the Cross,
He Suffered for Me

Let us run with endurance the race God has set before us. We do this by keeping our eyes on Jesus, the champion who initiates and perfects our faith. Because of the joy awaiting him, he endured the cross, disregarding its shame. Now he is seated in the place of honor beside God's throne.

HEBREWS 12:1–2

Have you ever done any long-distance running? I was always blown away by my peers in school who chose to be on the cross-country team. I thought they were nuts, because I've always disliked long-distance running. But secretly I was in awe of their endurance, their ability to withstand hardship or stress and come through it still standing!

The writer of Hebrews encourages us to do that very thing in life, to "run with endurance the race God has set before us." But then the writer tells us to look to Jesus as our inspiration. Jesus endured the cross, despising the shame and taking the weight of our sin on His shoulders. He is the only one who could do it because He is the author and finisher of our faith. And what's more, He did it with joy. Jesus endured the cross, with all its pain and with all its suffering, so that you and I might have joy and hope that is eternal.

Jesus, words fail to convey my gratitude for all that You endured on the cross for me!

What Do You See When You Look in the Mirror?

Don't judge by his appearance or height, for I have rejected him. The LORD doesn't see things the way you see them. People judge by outward appearance, but the LORD looks at the heart.

1 SAMUEL 16:7

It's funny, but when most of us look in the mirror our first reaction is negative. We think, *My hair is messy* or *I have bags under my eyes* or something similar. Rare is the day when we are actually satisfied with our outward appearance.

Even though our society places a great deal of importance on how we look on the outside, God's concern is how we look on the inside. Are you attractive on the inside? Is your heart free from sin and are your motives selfless? Only you and God know these things.

It is a pure heart and a genuine love for God that makes you attractive to Him. So if you want to live an authentic life of worship, you should examine yourself in the mirror, but closer now: past the blemishes and into your soul. Do you like what you see? Do you like who you are becoming on the inside? More importantly, does God like what He sees?

Lord, what do You see when You look into my heart? I confess I'm not thrilled with everything I see. There are ugly things in my life that need to be brought out into the light and dealt with. Have Your way in me today!

Perfect Worship

There is wonderful joy ahead, even though you must endure many trials for a little while. These trials will show that your faith is genuine. It is being tested as fire tests and purifies gold—though your faith is far more precious than mere gold.

1 PETER 1:6–7

In the book of James the author encourages us, "When troubles of any kind come your way, consider it an opportunity for great joy. For you know that when your faith is tested, your endurance has a chance to grow. So let it grow, for when your endurance is fully developed, you will be perfect and complete, needing nothing" (James 1:2–4).

The trials of life are tests of our faith. These tests produce patience in us: patience to walk through the fire so that we come out polished and perfected by the Master. Just as a master silversmith removes the dross from the silver in order to perfect his product, so the Master of the universe must send us through a fire or two to perfect our faith and our trust in Him. It can be painful, and no doubt it tests our patience, but God loves us too much to simply leave us the way we are. He wants us to be complete: perfect worshipers in His eyes.

Thank You, Father, that You love me too much to leave me the way I am. Help me not to resent the trials, knowing that You're at work and Your plan is perfect.

Worship God as a Family

Commit yourselves wholeheartedly to these words of mine. Tie them to your hands and wear them on your forehead as reminders. Teach them to your children. Talk about them when you are at home and when you are on the road, when you are going to bed and when you are getting up.

DEUTERONOMY 11:18–19

You've heard it said, "The family that prays together stays together." And honestly, it's true. It's hard to stay angry with each other and to fight openly when the Word of God is open before you and you are kneeling to pray.

If you aren't meeting with your family for regular times of prayer, Bible study, and devotion, I encourage you to begin as soon as you can. It will not only help you grow closer together, but it will also help ground you in the Word of God so that you will have strength throughout your days to live for Him.

Pick a verse that you can all learn together for the week and come up with fun ways to explore God's work in your lives. Take advantage of those moments of candid conversations so that you become the spiritual motivator of your family and a godly example to your children. And more than anything, work hard to discipline yourself to live a genuine life of worship at home in regular mundane activities.

Lord, help me to put this into practice in my home!

Worship Christ
for Who He Truly Is

God elevated him to the place of highest honor and gave him the name above all other names, that at the name of Jesus every knee should bow, in heaven and on earth and under the earth, and every tongue declare that Jesus Christ is Lord, to the glory of God the Father.

PHILIPPIANS 2:9–11

In Philippians 2, Paul tells us that a day is coming when every living creature will bow before Jesus in worship. By this he doesn't mean that everyone and everything will bow in universal salvation, but rather they will bow in universal subjugation. One day, every individual will face the Lord Jesus, and when that happens, they will have no choice but to acknowledge Him as King of kings and Lord of lords.

So here's a question for you today: Since we will all bow our knees in worship at some point, why not live our lives in honor and reverence to King Jesus now? It's not as though He is unloving and uncaring, or that the abundant joy He offers now is miserable drudgery! He is the author of hope and the giver of life! In Jesus is the fullness of true happiness.

So enjoy His presence today. Don't wait for the glories of heaven to discover the wonder of worship. Start right now by falling on your knees and giving your heart to Him in praise.

My King and my Lord, I bow before You today in worship. You are worthy of all my praise!

Is Your Worship Upside Down?

Yours, O LORD, is the greatness, the power, the glory, the victory, and the majesty. Everything in the heavens and on earth is yours, O LORD, and this is your kingdom.

I CHRONICLES 29:11

In Romans 1:20, Paul explains that there are certain "invisible qualities" or signs of God that can be clearly seen by all mankind, thereby giving none of us an excuse for not giving Him glory. As *The Message* version puts it, "People knew God perfectly well, but when they didn't treat him like God, refusing to worship him, they trivialized themselves into silliness and confusion so that there was neither sense nor direction left in their lives. They pretended to know it all"—yet in reality they knew nothing of the truth and grace of God. So the result was a trade: They traded the glory of the Creator, who holds the whole world in His hands, for the elements of creation. To be sure, the beauty of a mountain or a tree gives testimony to the glory of God. But it is not an object to be worshiped itself. That's upside-down worship. That is worshiping a man-made god instead of the God who made man.

So today, make sure your worship is right-side up. Worship the one and only Creator God, who made you and loves you and gave Himself for you. He is the only hope you have.

Creator God, save me from falling into the trap of worshiping the things You've made rather than You Yourself.

What Do You Live For?

My purpose is to give them a rich and satisfying life.

JOHN 10:10

Artists live to create that one masterpiece. Authors live to create that one life's work. Athletes live to win championships. But what do you live for? Maybe today you don't feel like you have anything to live for; you're just existing. Or even worse, you feel like you're dying. Don't be like that author who wrote, "First, I was dying to finish high school and start college. Then I was dying to finish college and start working. Then I was dying to marry and have children. Then I was dying for my children to grow old enough for school so I could return to work. Then I was dying to retire. And now, I am dying . . . and suddenly I realize I forgot to live."

When worshiping Jesus becomes our all-consuming passion, it becomes the life-giving force behind all we do. Worship becomes a lifestyle of loving Jesus. And Jesus is the one who gives us life! First John 5:12 reminds us, "Whoever has the Son has life; whoever does not have God's Son does not have life." True living starts by doing what you were created to do: worship God. We were made to live for Him. Try it; you will discover just how fulfilling this life can be!

Jesus, You are the one who gives me a reason to get up in the morning. Life with You is an incredible adventure!

How Is It with Your Soul?

All Scripture is inspired by God and is useful to teach us what is true and to make us realize what is wrong in our lives. It corrects us when we are wrong and teaches us to do what is right. God uses it to prepare and equip his people to do every good work.

2 TIMOTHY 3:16–17

How is it with your soul?" That's a question the old Wesleyans used to ask each other when they got together. It's an intriguing question that probes beyond the surface and gets to the heart of the matter quickly. It's a question that starts from the inside and works its way out.

Our soul is, by far, the most precious possession we have. Just as we need to tend to our bodies and get physical exercise, so we need to tend to the health of our souls if we want to be spiritually strong. Begin by drawing near to the only One who can help you: Jesus. Dive into the Word of God with purpose and direction. Set your feet on a path of spiritual growth. The resources are endless, but start with the simple reading of the Word of God and with simply pouring your heart out to Him in prayer. Doing that each day will improve the condition of your soul for eternity.

Help me, Father, to be diligent in tending to the health of my soul. Show me what steps I need to take to do better.

The Presence of God: No Better Place to Be

Moses said to him, "If your Presence does not go with us, do not send us up from here."

EXODUS 33:15 NIV

When God called Moses to deliver His people from slavery in Egypt, Moses gave a typical response: "Me? I don't think I'm up to this task. Isn't there someone else?" God promised Moses His presence would go with him. But Moses wanted something more, something tangible.

Now fast-forward to Mount Sinai. Moses has delivered the people from Egypt, and he is up on the mountain receiving God's handwritten Ten Commandments. Down below, the people have rebelled and the Lord is furious! But Moses intercedes on their behalf and God decides to spare them—with one exception. His presence will no longer accompany them in the wilderness. To which Moses replies: "If your Presence does not go with us, do not send us up from here."

Isn't it interesting that early on, Moses had to have something in addition to God's presence in order to have the faith to move, but now all that matters to Moses is to be in the presence of God? Nothing else. If you and I could ever get to that point in our walk with God, there's no telling how He could use us to change the world.

Lord, may I get to the place in my walk with You that You are all I need.

How Passionate Is Your Worship?

Whom have I in heaven but you? I desire you more than anything on earth. My health may fail, and my spirit may grow weak, but God remains the strength of my heart; he is mine forever.

PSALM 73:25–26

We worship what we're passionate about. And we're passionate about what we worship. If you don't believe me, go to a football or baseball game. There you will see an incredibly accurate depiction of the right kind of worship; it's just worship of the wrong god. We show loyalty and dedication to our favorite team by wearing our team's colors. We make sacrifices as we spend enormous sums of money to buy our tickets. We feel anticipation and excitement, so much so that we're willing to get to the game three hours early and park a mile away just to make sure we don't miss anything. But most of all we express passion. We passionately praise our team when they do well, and we passionately mourn when they lose.

Can you imagine what our lives would be like if we approached worshiping God with the same passion with which we cheer on our teams? What would that look like? Think about the team you're passionate about and how you express your support. Now consider how you can pour that same passion into worshiping God. He deserves our passionate worship.

I confess, Father, that I don't always worship You with the same level of passion I use to follow other things in my life. I need Your help to change that!

Poor in Spirit, Rich in Worship

God blesses those who are poor and realize their need for him, for the Kingdom of Heaven is theirs.

MATTHEW 5:3

I'll never forget standing at the rim of a huge garbage pit in Guatemala looking down and seeing dozens of villagers rummaging through the garbage for something to eat. It absolutely broke my heart. Houses made of sticks and plastic from garbage bags, no shoes, no clean water, and very little food. And yet, when we held a worship service in the church we'd built for them, the place filled up with many of those same villagers. And they radiated the joy of the Lord.

That's the wonderful thing about the all-inclusive good news of Jesus. You aren't excluded because you're poor, and you aren't included because you're rich. Both rich and poor must humble themselves in His presence to receive His salvation. We must all be poor in spirit.

What does it mean to be "poor in spirit"? It means you have come to the place in your life where you realize you are nothing and have nothing without God. You realize you are helpless and hopeless without the rescuing hand of almighty God. There is no arrogance or self-sufficiency left in you. When we get to this place in our lives, we are poor in spirit and will inherit the Kingdom of God. So rid yourself of yourself, and lean only on Jesus today.

O Lord, I'm nothing apart from You. All my hope is in You.

Worship Wherever You Are

The LORD is my strength and my song; he has given me victory. This is my God, and I will praise him—my father's God, and I will exalt him!

EXODUS 15:2

Sitting on a plane early one morning, I happened to look out the window just as the sun was rising above the thick, cloud-covered horizon. It was one of the most spectacular sights I've ever seen. In that moment, I was reminded that we worship a God who is both mighty and merciful. He is mighty as Creator, Ruler, Sustainer, and King. Yet He is merciful as Savior, Healer, Provider, and Friend.

The cloud cover made me think of my life, so riddled with doubt, sin, murky vision, and lack of faith. But the beauty of that sun rising above the clouds reminded me of just how faithful God is to carry me out of all the dark things in my life. I witnessed a rising sun, but that moment drove me to worship the risen Son and to praise Him in that early hour for the salvation and grace I have received despite my position of unworthiness.

Today, wherever you are, take a moment and remember what Jesus has done for you. His mercies are new each morning, and His grace is sufficient to carry you through it all. He is King, and He is Friend—worthy of all worship, deserving of all praise!

Jesus, thank You for all that You've done for me. Thank You for fresh mercy and all-sufficient grace.

Worship with a Lifestyle of Holiness

Live as God's obedient children. Don't slip back into your old ways of living to satisfy your own desires. . . . You must be holy in everything you do, just as God who chose you is holy.

1 PETER 1:14–15

Holiness is a two-sided coin. On one side of the coin is our position of holiness. There's absolutely nothing we've done to deserve our salvation in Christ. He accomplished everything for us because of His sacrifice on the cross and because He conquered sin, death, hell, and the grave with His resurrection. So we are blessed to be eternally sealed in a position of holiness simply because of the grace of Jesus.

However, the flip side of that coin is that holiness is also a process. It is the personal responsibility of every believer to pursue a life of holiness. The Bible is very clear about the fact that we should constantly be in a state of growing closer to Jesus, striving toward an intimate walk with Him. "Let us cleanse ourselves from everything that can defile our body or spirit. And let us work toward complete holiness because we fear God" (2 Corinthians 7:1).

So think on these things today. Take comfort in knowing that God sees you as holy through the sacrifice of His Son. But also, take responsibility in disciplining yourself to pursue a lifestyle of holiness.

Thank You, Jesus, that in You I'm made holy. Help me by Your Spirit to pursue a lifestyle of holiness.

Becoming a Worship Leader

Be an example to all believers in what you say, in the way you live, in your love, your faith, and your purity.

1 TIMOTHY 4:12

Sociologists tell us that because of social networks, e-mail, work environments, and numerous other outlets, each one of us will have a direct influence on the lives of at least ten thousand people over our lifetime. That's a lot of influence! The question is, what kind of influence will it be?

Leadership is influence. Like it or not, all of us are leaders to a certain degree. Look around you—someone is in your direct line of influence. You are a leader of someone. Are you their worship leader as well? Of course I don't mean whether or not you can sing and play guitar. I mean, are you showing them an example of what it means to live a life of worship? I pray you are, because there is no other purpose in life higher than that.

As a child of God, begin to see yourself as a worship leader. If leadership is influence, then why not expand that and glorify God with it? It will take discipline and humility to allow Him to shape your heart. And it will take surrendering your will to His. But just think of the endless ways in which God wants to use you as a leader.

Heavenly Father, may I be ever mindful that You have placed certain people in my sphere of influence. May I be a faithful leader who points them to You!

Worship with Detail

I plead with you to give your bodies to God because of all he has done for you. Let them be a living and holy sacrifice—the kind he will find acceptable. This is truly the way to worship him.

ROMANS 12:1

Have you ever read the book of Exodus? You'll discover in chapters 25 through 30 just how detailed the God we worship really is. He was extremely detailed in how He wanted His people to worship Him, giving them precise instructions on how to construct the tabernacle, how to carry out sacrifices, and so on. And although we now live under grace and under the new covenant because of Jesus, God has still made it clear how we are to worship Him. A starting point is Romans 12:1, where we are told to present our bodies as a living sacrifice. We are to live holy and acceptable in His sight.

Always remember, the God of the Old Testament and the God of the New Testament are the same God. He has not changed and He never will. But because of Jesus we no longer have to follow the detailed regiment of the Old Covenant. Instead, we are to live every moment in detailed obedience to Him. Simply put, fall in love with Jesus and worship Him in every little detail of your life.

Father, I surrender myself to You as a living sacrifice. Have Your way in every area of my life.

Worship Jesus as Healer

Let all that I am praise the LORD; with my whole heart, I will praise his holy name. Let all that I am praise the LORD; may I never forget the good things he does for me. He forgives all my sins and heals all my diseases.

PSALM 103:1–3

One of the great miracles Jesus performed takes place in Luke 17, but it is also one of the saddest stories.

Ten lepers were living outside the city of Jerusalem. They were forced to live outside the city gates because they were required to quarantine themselves as diseased people. When they saw Jesus, they cried out to Him, "Jesus, Master, have mercy on us!" (Luke 17:13). Jesus saw them and had pity on them. He told them to go and show the priest that they had been healed, and as they went, they were made whole. Can you imagine their excitement and the overwhelming sense of healing? Their lives were doomed until Jesus healed them. But sadly, only one of them returned to thank Jesus. The rest went on their merry way.

Isn't that just like us? We are so blessed in so many ways, but often we take our blessings for granted and don't show the gratitude to our Lord that He deserves. I encourage you today to list the many ways God has blessed you and then tell Him how grateful you are!

Forgive me, Lord, for failing to show You the gratitude You deserve. Today I thank You for . . .

Worship Jesus as Provider

There is one who scatters, yet increases more; and there is one who withholds more than is right, but it leads to poverty.

PROVERBS 11:24 NKJV

Are you concerned about being able to provide for your family? Or maybe you're worried today about simply providing for yourself. When a job is lost or we have unexpected expenses like a car breakdown or medical bills, then the reality of having to provide for ourselves or others can hit hard.

Interestingly, the most famous verse about God supplying our needs in the Bible is actually about God supplying our needs after we have provided for others. In Philippians 4:19, Paul wrote, "My God shall supply all your need according to His riches in glory by Christ Jesus" (NKJV). He wrote this to the Philippians because they had first provided for him financially. "At the moment I have all I need—and more! I am generously supplied with the gifts you sent me with Epaphroditus" (Philippians 4:18).

Jesus urged us to "seek the Kingdom of God above all else, and live righteously, and he will give you everything you need" (Matthew 6:33). It is a solid biblical principle that when we focus our energy and attention on God first, then others second, He meets our needs and blesses us. We cannot outgive God. He will always give back to us more than we could ever imagine.

I trust Your Word, Lord. Increase my faith to believe in Your provision as I seek first Your kingdom.

Worship Jesus as Creator

Acknowledge that the LORD is God! He made us, and we are his. We are his people, the sheep of his pasture. Enter his gates with thanksgiving; go into his courts with praise. Give thanks to him and praise his name. For the LORD is good. His unfailing love continues forever, and his faithfulness continues to each generation.

PSALM 100:3–5

Colossians 1 is one of my favorite chapters in the Bible. In this chapter, Paul spends several moments just exalting Jesus. He reminds us of the position Jesus holds in light of all of creation: the preeminent place. He is supreme over all. In fact, the Word says, "He is the image of the invisible God, the firstborn over all creation. For by Him all things were created that are in heaven and that are on earth, visible and invisible, whether thrones or dominions or principalities or powers. All things were created through Him and for Him" (Colossians 1:15–16 NKJV). Paul wrote elsewhere: "Everything comes from him and exists by his power and is intended for his glory" (Romans 11:36).

Those "things" include you and me. You and I were created by Jesus and for Jesus. After reading these verses, could there be any doubt left in your mind as to why you exist on this earth? We are created by Jesus to bring glory and honor to Jesus and to live a life that honors and worships only Jesus!

Jesus, I am on this earth to glorify You. Help me to live my life accordingly!

Worship Jesus as Friend

No longer do I call you servants, for a servant does not know what his master is doing; but I have called you friends, for all things that I heard from My Father I have made known to you.

JOHN 15:15 NKJV

When it comes down to it, most of us can count our closest friends on one hand. And none of us can deny that there's a difference between close acquaintances and close friends. As someone once said, "A friend is the one coming in the door when everyone else is walking out."

Friends stick close—through the good times and the bad. Friends love us in spite of our faults. Friends love us unconditionally. That's why I love the Bible's description of Jesus: He is the "friend who sticks closer than a brother" (Proverbs 18:24 NKJV). Jesus stands behind you, believes in you, and will encourage you despite what you're going through. He said Himself, "I will never fail you. I will never abandon you" (Hebrews 13:5).

So why don't we spend more time getting to know the most faithful friend we could ever have? I encourage you today, as a worshiper of Jesus, to spend some time developing your friendship with King Jesus. It may amaze you to know that it gives Him great joy when you step into His presence!

I couldn't ask for a better friend than You, Jesus. What do You want to talk about today?

Worship Jesus as Sustainer

The LORD is my strength and shield. I trust him with all my heart. He helps me, and my heart is filled with joy. I burst out in songs of thanksgiving.

PSALM 28:7

Psalm 54:4 is one of my favorite verses: "Behold, God is my helper; the Lord is the sustainer of my soul" (NASB). What does it mean when the Bible says the Lord is our Sustainer? It means that He holds all things together. The entire universe is held in His hands.

Look at Colossians 1:17: "He is before all things, and in him all things hold together" (NIV). In this verse He is referring to Jesus Christ, the ruler and savior of the world. Isn't it comforting to know that the entire cosmos, with all its chaos, is held together in the hands of almighty Jesus? He is our helper in times of need, our teacher in times of confusion, our comforter in times of worry, our fortress in times of insecurity, and our guide when we have lost our way. Our God is so worthy of our praise.

So the next time you worry about whether or not God can handle your situation or you watch the news and worry about the future, be reminded that you were created by almighty God, the ruler and the sustainer of the universe!

Almighty God, in Your hands I have nothing to fear. Thank You for being my trustworthy sustainer.

Worship Jesus as Deliverer

If the Son makes you free, you shall be free indeed.

JOHN 8:36 NKJV

Imagine what it would be like to be imprisoned by ISIS rebels, held in a dungeon or cave in a remote part of Iraq, with no food, no rest, and no one to come to your rescue. There are many in that situation today, and we need to pray desperately for them. But then imagine if you were suddenly released. How amazing would that feeling of freedom be?

In essence, this is what it is like in our spirits when we receive the forgiveness and the salvation of our Lord Jesus. He sets us free: delivers us from the shackles of sin and the shame of our past. No longer do they have any hold on us. And here's the best part: You didn't have to do anything to earn it. God's forgiveness rescues you from the bondage of guilt and sets you free to praise Him with a lifestyle that glorifies Him. This deliverance alone gives us great reason to celebrate in worship of Him.

Be encouraged by Galatians 5:1: "Stand fast therefore in the liberty by which Christ has made us free, and do not be entangled again with a yoke of bondage" (NKJV).

Strong Deliverer, I praise You and thank You for setting me free from the hold that sin had on me, for granting me Your wonderful salvation.

Worship That Makes a Difference

Whether you eat or drink, or whatever you do, do all to the glory of God.

1 CORINTHIANS 10:31 NKJV

My son Cooper and I were walking the beach one November day. As we walked, we would drag our feet in the sand near the water and make little trenches. But those trenches didn't last long. The waves soon came in and washed them all away, leaving no trace.

It made me think of the fleetingness of life. Our lives are so short. Here today, gone tomorrow. I thought of how the lives of those who live in the moment, seeking the temporary pleasures of sin, are like those trenches we dug in the sand that were soon swept away by the waves. Eventually, they will die and will leave no lasting, positive imprint on society or legacy in the kingdom of God.

I don't know about you, but I want my life to count for something, both now and for eternity. I don't want to just leave a footprint in the sand, only to have it washed away with the next wave. I want to make a difference in the lives of my children and my culture. I can start by living each and every moment for the glory of God.

Father, I want to leave behind a legacy for Your kingdom. Help me to live every moment for You and make a godly impression on those who come behind me.

Worship While You Play

I decided there is nothing better than to enjoy food and drink and to find satisfaction in work. Then I realized that these pleasures are from the hand of God. For who can eat or enjoy anything apart from him? God gives wisdom, knowledge, and joy to those who please him.

ECCLESIASTES 2:24–26

Did you know you can worship the Lord while playing golf, or boating on the lake, or taking a walk in your neighborhood? Of course you can! Because, as you've heard me say many times, worship is simply you and me loving God.

So whether it is during work or play or spending time with our loved ones, or even our enemies for that matter, worship is displayed through the motivation of our hearts, the actions of our bodies, and the thoughts in our minds. If those are intact and bringing honor to God, then we can certainly worship Him as we participate in the lighter side of life, our hobbies or our games.

We just need to be careful, as our fun stuff can easily consume us. Trust me, I've made that mistake before. You may have heard it said, "We worship our work, work at our play, and play at our worship." May God help us to have the spiritual discipline we need to keep our worship, work, and play balanced and in line, and we will discover that worship and play can coexist.

God, help me to honor You and worship You in every area of my life including, and perhaps especially, my play.

Worship the Lord Right Now!

How do you know what your life will be like tomorrow? Your life is like the morning fog—it's here a little while, then it's gone.

JAMES 4:14

We are here on this earth for just a short time, and then we are gone. Since we are here for only a little while, my question is, what are you doing with the precious time you have?

Have you ever noticed that so much of our time is spent planning what we will do in the future? But the apostle James encourages us to think about what we're doing right now. He reminds us that we don't know what will happen tomorrow. Only God knows our future. We must approach each day with a surrendered will to follow His plan.

Trusting in God is the only real way we can prepare ourselves for tomorrow because He is the only one who controls it. We don't have much time to begin with, so we should spend that time doing what God created us to do: worship. By this I mean that every aspect of our lives can be an act that glorifies our Creator. Is there a better way to spend your precious days than knowing everything you do is motivated by a sincere desire to honor the Lord? In turn, you bless the Father with a life well-lived, and He blesses you for living a life that is pleasing to Him.

Father, help me to make the most of the time I have left on this earth.

Why Are We Here on This Earth?

O people, the LORD has told you what is good, and this is what he requires of you: to do what is right, to love mercy, and to walk humbly with your God.

MICAH 6:8

We see it in Hollywood all too often, where wealthy, successful, beautiful stars end up dying in their own misery. It's truly sad. But the reason so many end up this way is that they've missed the point of their existence. They suffered from a feeling of purposelessness.

We need to remember that God never does anything without a purpose. And His purpose in creating us is so that we would worship Him and fellowship with Him. His plan was a perfect one. Then sin messed it all up. But even though sin has blurred the minds of so many people throughout history, our purpose for existing hasn't changed. We exist on this earth for one purpose: to glorify God. We are to know Him and make Him known.

If we want to live a truly fulfilling life, one that is full of hope, purpose, and adventure, then it begins when our worship is rightly aligned with the only One who is worthy of that worship—the Lord God Almighty. Don't let sin cloud your vision and purpose for life. You are made in His image, so fulfill your purpose in life by living to worship Him.

I'm grateful, Lord, for the purpose my life holds, for the fulfillment that comes from worshiping You and living for You.

The Songs of Worship

Be filled with the Holy Spirit, singing psalms and hymns and spiritual songs among yourselves, and making music to the Lord in your hearts. And give thanks for everything to God the Father in the name of our Lord Jesus Christ.

EPHESIANS 5:18–20

To worship the Lord is our primary responsibility in life. Worship is loving God with all our heart, soul, mind, and strength. Many of us express that worship by way of song. And over the last twenty years or so, we have witnessed a sort of worship revolution in our churches. This is due in large part to the many wonderful songwriters and singers who have delivered new expressions of worship to the platforms of our churches. Many of these songs are simply Scripture put to music, so even though the sound is new, the message is ancient and true.

I encourage you today to embrace these new songs of praise, as many of them are incredibly uplifting and will speak to your heart. At the same time, I encourage you not to forsake the great, timeless songs of our faith that have touched the hearts of countless souls for many generations.

These songs, both old and new, both hymn and chorus, are just one avenue through which God speaks to us and draws us closer to Him. Listen to them. Sing them. They will change your life!

I lift my songs of praise to You today, beautiful Savior!

Worship with Balance and Rhythm

Jesus said, "Let's go off by ourselves to a quiet place and rest awhile." He said this because there were so many people coming and going that Jesus and his apostles didn't even have time to eat.

MARK 6:31

The longer I live, the more I am learning that life has a certain rhythm to it. My life has never been one of routine. Instead, it's been greatly out of balance and way too busy most of the time. I used to wear that busyness as a badge of honor. But as I grow older, I'm realizing that I've developed some awful habits. I can't sit still, I can't slow down, and when I try, I feel guilty about it.

But the problem is, all motion and no rest eventually produces activity without accomplishment. When we're depleted, we lose our way. All of us live our lives to a certain rhythm. We all have routines that we go through every day. Our universe has a rhythm to it as well. There is the rhythm of the tide and the rhythm of the sun. There should also be a rhythm in our lives to work and to rest.

We have to create space in our days in order to generate productivity in our lives. So today, take some time to consider the rhythm of your life.

Lord, enable me to find balance and rhythm in my life. Help me to give myself permission to rest, for it's a gift from You.

Mercy for You Means Mercy for Me

God is so rich in mercy, and he loved us so much, that even though we were dead because of our sins, he gave us life when he raised Christ from the dead. (It is only by God's grace that you have been saved!)

EPHESIANS 2:4–5

We have all experienced mercy at some point. I remember when I disappeared from the house as a sixth-grader and no one in my family knew where I was. I was just down the street playing with some friends, but I had failed to tell anyone where I was going. So when my parents finally found me, they were incredibly upset but joyful at the same time. In fact, they were so happy I had been found that they didn't even punish me.

That's mercy—not getting what we deserve. Jesus said, "Blessed are the merciful, for they shall obtain mercy" (Matthew 5:7 NKJV). Those who give mercy are blessed because they have chosen to forgive and forget instead of giving in to hostility and anger. And because they have shown mercy to others, Jesus promises they will receive mercy in return. We learn to forgive because we have been forgiven. We are able to show mercy because mercy has been given to us.

As a worshiping servant of Jesus, what does His love require you to do today?

Jesus, help me to be quick to extend mercy to those around me as You have so graciously extended mercy to me.

Worship When You Are Lonely

Listen to the LORD who created you. . . . "Do not be afraid, for I have ransomed you. I have called you by name; you are mine. When you go through deep waters, I will be with you. When you go through rivers of difficulty, you will not drown."

ISAIAH 43:1–2

Have you ever been lonely? I asked that question one night during a concert, and for the first time all night, a little teenage girl sitting in the front row lifted up her head, looked me in the eye, and nodded her head. Her look shook me to the core.

Loneliness is a real issue for many people. In a world of seven billion people, thousands of mega-cities, and hundreds of social networks, one of the biggest problems we face in this technological age is loneliness. But as God's children, we can rest in the comfort of God's promises. He never fails us. He will not turn His back on us.

If you're feeling all alone, rest assured that you aren't. You have God's Spirit within you, and He holds you in His hands. And do you want to know the best part? He will never let you go! He will carry you through it. So if you are lonely today, turn your eyes upon Jesus and worship Him. He still has His eyes on you as a loving Father and His arms around you as a faithful Friend. Worship Him through this lonely time.

Faithful Friend, thank You that I'm never alone!

Worship the God of Peace

I am leaving you with a gift—peace of mind and heart. And the peace I give is a gift the world cannot give. So don't be troubled or afraid.

JOHN 14:27

Over seven hundred years before the birth of Christ, the prophet Isaiah foretold that Jesus, the coming Savior, would be called the Prince of Peace. At the time Isaiah wrote these words, the people of Israel were under threat of war and in a period of unrest because of an ungodly king. So the thought of peace not only calmed the people, but it also brought hope to them.

Now, God's kingdom of peace is not established by making war. Instead, the peace that God gives is an eternal, indescribable peace that only comes through faith in the Prince of Peace. That peace is available to you today. No matter what you are going through, whether it's a health problem, financial woes, or the loss of a loved one, Jesus is the only one who can bring you peace. Perhaps you're at war within your own soul because you aren't sure what you believe about God. Whatever it is, the answer is still the same: Jesus is the only answer. Seek Him. Trust Him. Worship Him. He will bring you peace.

Jesus, Prince of Peace, You are the answer I seek. In You alone I find rest and peace when my soul is troubled.

Worship the Lord in Truth

The time is coming—indeed it's here now—when true worshipers will worship the Father in spirit and in truth. The Father is looking for those who will worship him that way. For God is Spirit, so those who worship him must worship in spirit and truth.

JOHN 4:23–24

In John 4, we read about Jesus's encounter with the Samaritan woman at Jacob's well. Throughout the course of His conversation with her, He revealed to her that the location of our worship is not nearly as important as the heart of our worship.

At the heart of our worship lie two important elements: spirit and truth. To worship in spirit means we worship God from the depths of our souls. It's not about a place or an object. God is Spirit; His Holy Spirit dwells within us, so our worship must come from our spirits as well. Worship is beyond the physical realm. Worship is a spiritual matter.

But worship is also an intellectual matter. We must worship in truth. I implore you today to study and meditate on the truth of God's Word. It has stood the test of time and proven to be true time and time again. Live by its principles. Know what you believe and why you believe it. Worship Jesus today in spirit and in truth!

I worship You, God, from the depths of my soul. As I dig into Your Word, help me to live by its principles and so worship You in truth.

Worship Jesus,
Name above All Names

There is salvation in no one else! God has given no other name under heaven by which we must be saved.

ACTS 4:12

Everyone has a name. Every name has a meaning. And every name assigns an identity. It tells us a little about who we are. Have you ever taken the time to discover what your name means?

What does the name of Jesus mean to you? To the disciple John, the name of Jesus meant beloved brother and loving friend. To Peter, Jesus's name represented patience and the rock of salvation. To Mary Magdalene, His name represented the God of a second chance, so worthy of worship. To Pilate, Jesus's name meant the one who was innocent and astoundingly strong. But what does the name of Jesus mean to you? Is He merely a prophet, priest, or Jewish rabbi? Or is He Savior and King, Ruler and Master? Does the name of Jesus draw some emotion out of you, as He is the giver of life, love, joy, and peace? Do you realize today that He knows your name? He fashioned you before you were born. He knows all about you—your hurts, your habits, even the number of hairs on your head. And since He knows you so well and loves you enough to die for you, take the time to get to know Him, to love Him, to worship Him.

I'm so glad You know my name, heavenly Father. Now I want to get to know You better.

Worship God with a Christian Worldview

Be innocent as babies when it comes to evil, but be mature in understanding matters of this kind.

I CORINTHIANS 14:20

I'm trying to teach my kids to have a Christian worldview. In other words, I want them to know their culture, to be able to communicate with their culture, but not to get sucked into the temptation and the sin of our culture. I want my children to be in the world, but not of it. This means that I must teach them to be "wise as serpents and harmless as doves" (Matthew 10:16 NKJV).

How we read the paper, watch the news, or interpret culture should all filter through our Christian worldview. In other words, we should look at all reality with the mind of Christ. As worshipers we need to learn what it means to live wisely in this world and to develop a godly love for our culture. Not to embrace the things of this world, but rather the humanity of this world.

So today, let's allow the actions of Jesus to change our view of how we treat others. Let's allow our meditation on His words to inspire us to reach our culture with the hope we have within us. And let's look at each person the way Jesus would look at them.

Father, help me to engage with my culture in a way that honors You and shines the light of Jesus.

Grace-Filled Worshipers

God's law was given so that all people could see how sinful they were. But as people sinned more and more, God's wonderful grace became more abundant.

ROMANS 5:20

Law and grace. We desperately need both. When Jesus came, He wasn't against the law, but He did disagree with what people were being taught about it. The law shows us how imperfect we are. The grace of Jesus forgives that imperfection. The purpose of the law is to bring us into a positive relationship with God and our fellow man. The grace of Jesus bridges that broken relationship between God and man. Obeying the law of God is all about what we do. The grace of God is about who we are. We are sinners saved by the love of Christ.

There are those within the Church who teach nothing but grace and love, and there are those who teach nothing but law and legalism. But we need a balanced understanding of the two. The truth is, we need the law; it teaches us right from wrong. And we need grace; it is what saves us from our human inability to obey the law of God completely.

Conviction without compassion is damning. Compassion without conviction is dangerous. But conviction with compassion—now that's dynamic. As worshipers, the law of God is our guide, but grace is our motive and our salvation.

Thank You for the law, dear Father, and thank You for grace. Help me to find a godly balance of the two in my life.

How Do You Spend Your Time?

Teach us to realize the brevity of life, so that we may grow in wisdom.

PSALM 90:12

The phrase "spending time" is rich with meaning. First of all, to spend anything means it's going to cost you something. And time is the most expensive and important commodity we have in life. Why? Because every second we spend is a moment we will never get back. Once a moment is past, it's gone forever.

The Bible reminds us that life is fleeting. It's like the grass: it grows and then fades away. We all start life with a certain amount of time in our account. None of us know how much time we start with, so we don't know how much time we have left. We must cherish and take advantage of every moment given to us by our Lord. We should enjoy life to its fullest and, as Ephesians 5:15–16 says, "Be careful how you live. Don't live like fools, but like those who are wise. Make the most of every opportunity in these evil days."

Each day is a precious gift. Choose your moments wisely. And the wisest way you can spend your time is by worshiping Jesus. It is with this time that you truly learn how to live a life well spent.

Lord, I want to spend the time I have left on this earth worshiping You and living for You!

Worship One Step at a Time

Blessed is the man who walks not in the counsel of the ungodly, nor stands in the path of sinners, nor sits in the seat of the scornful; but his delight is in the law of the LORD, and in His law he meditates day and night.

PSALM 1:1–2 NKJV

Most accomplishments in life require a progression of some sort. For instance, LeBron James didn't become the basketball player he is now after one shot. It took a process of slow progression—one step at a time to greatness. Most of us look at progression as a positive thing, and it is. But if we aren't careful, we can progress backward, or regress, as well. It's subtle, but it can happen so easily.

This is the progression the psalmist warns us about in Psalm 1. Those who walk around sin long enough always end up succumbing to it because sin always takes you further than you wanted to go, keeps you longer than you ever planned to stay, and costs you more than you could ever afford to pay.

We must be careful not to walk into the traps that so easily beset us, whether it's a simple button on our computer, a remote in our hand, or a second glance in the wrong direction. Once you walk down that path, it gets more and more difficult to turn around. So walk intentionally today with a lifestyle of worship.

Father, may I be so busy seeking You and delighting in You that earthly temptations lose their allure.

Do Distractions Hinder Your Worship?

To me, living means living for Christ, and dying is even better.

PHILIPPIANS 1:21

Distractions are everywhere. That's why we have to constantly remind ourselves where our priorities lie. Of course our priorities should focus on the things that are most important, but sometimes distractions keep us from doing that.

I encourage you today to start with the basics. Who are you and why are you here? You are God's very own and your first priority is to worship Him. Everything else falls under that priority. The problem is, so many things vie for our attention and affection these days that it's easy to become distracted in our worship and service to God.

An undivided heart is a heart that is rid of distractions. It means that there's no war going on inside of you over whom you will serve and whom you will worship. What is it today that is distracting your lifestyle of worship? Consider these things today. As you move throughout the day, let everything you do take place under the umbrella of worship. With this mind-set, you will discover that your conversations, the way you spend your money, and the way you spend your time will change. Distractions will come, but hold fast to that first priority. It will mold you into the worshiper God created you to be.

Lord, show me the things in my life that are distracting me from worshiping You with a whole heart.

The Resurrection and the Life

Just as the Father gives life to those he raises from the dead, so the Son gives life to anyone he wants.

JOHN 5:21

I wish I could have been there to see Jesus call Lazarus from the grave. And I *really* wish I could have been there to see Lazarus walk out of that grave. He'd been dead for four days, and everyone in town was grieving his death. But Martha meets Jesus as He enters town and displays great faith when she tells Him that she still believes anything is possible with God. I believe that Martha's faith is one of the reasons Jesus responded with these words: "Your brother will rise again" (John 11:23). And then Jesus said, "I am the resurrection and the life" (John 11:25). In other words, "Death has no power over Me, even after it has done its deed."

He proved this with Lazarus, and soon after, He would prove it with His own resurrection. He holds the power of life and death in His hands. He is the only Way: the mediator between death and life eternal.

He is mighty in His power over death, and He is mighty because of His grace. His grace is broad enough to forgive every sin and sufficient to keep each of us held in His hands forever. So worship the resurrected Lord today!

I thank You and praise You, Jesus, for conquering death and giving me life eternal!

Embracing the Mystery of Worship

O Lord my God, you have performed many wonders for us. Your plans for us are too numerous to list. You have no equal. If I tried to recite all your wonderful deeds, I would never come to the end of them.

PSALM 40:5

If you're like me, you like things carved out for you in neat packages, plain to see, easy to understand. Unfortunately, that's just not the reality of our spiritual condition. Many times there is a mystery to the things of God. Often His Word is difficult to understand and His ways are hard to fathom.

But there's a verse in Scripture that really helps me when I question the mysteries. It reminds me that, although I may not understand what God is doing or why I'm going through something, He is in control and He is sovereign. That verse is Isaiah 55:8: "'My thoughts are nothing like your thoughts,' says the Lord. 'And my ways are far beyond anything you could imagine.'"

Let's face it, we will never fully grasp the mind of God. He is beyond our comprehension in every way, but He is also the one who knows it all, owns it all, created it all, and holds it all together. We can trust Him. And in our trusting Him, we worship Him.

Father, I trust You even when I don't understand what You're up to. You hold my world in Your hands and I am safe.

Worship with Integrity

The integrity of the upright will guide them, but the perversity of the unfaithful will destroy them.

PROVERBS 11:3 NKJV

The word *integrity* comes from the root word *integer*. An integer is any whole number, or a number that has no fraction. So a life of integrity is a life lived in wholeness or completeness. Let me put it this way. If I want to have a complete marriage, then I must be wholly committed. If I'm faithful to my wife 99 percent of the time, I am not completely faithful, which shatters my integrity with her.

People of integrity live consistently. So it goes with our lifestyle of worship. We must live lives of integrity. Whether it be in the company of many, or all alone in a hotel room, worshipers of integrity remain consistent in their pursuit of holiness. It is our responsibility to live for Jesus in all things, the big and the small. Even if it seems like a harmless little infraction, as believers we must maintain absolute integrity, both in public and in private.

You've heard it said before, but it bears repeating: "You are what you are when no one is looking." Worship the Lord with integrity and your hope will never falter. You'll find your life is more complete because of it. "May integrity and honesty protect me, for I put my hope in you" (Psalm 25:21).

O Lord, help me by Your Spirit to live a life of integrity!

Is Your Worship on Automatic?

I remind you to stir up the gift of God which is in you through the laying on of my hands. For God has not given us a spirit of fear, but of power and of love and of a sound mind.

2 TIMOTHY 1:6–7 NKJV

I love sweet tea. But just as much as I love sweet tea, I can't stand unsweetened tea. The difference, of course, is the sugar. But have you ever poured sugar into your tea and forgotten to stir it up? Technically, it *is* sweet tea. But experientially, it is *not* sweet. And so it is with our lives of worship. We have been given that greatest gift imaginable—salvation! But just as that sugar will settle at the bottom of the glass of tea if we don't stir it, we will become apathetic and complacent in our love for Jesus if we don't continually grow closer to Him.

Paul uses this imagery as he encourages young Timothy to "stir up the gift of God which is in you" (2 Timothy 1:6 NKJV). He was reminding Timothy and the rest of us that God has given us the spirit of power and love through His salvation and that those around us are in need of our passionate and dedicated service to the Lord. So get out of automatic, and let God stir you today so that you exude the sweet salvation that comes only from Jesus.

Jesus, save me from living on automatic. Stir my heart today and renew my passion.

Make an Appointment with God

I rise early, before the sun is up; I cry out for help and put my hope in your words. I stay awake through the night, thinking about your promise.

PSALM 119:147–148

Do you spend time with God? I mean real time, in prayer and study of His Word. Too often I've been guilty of skipping moments with the Lord, or just reading a verse or two to get the legalistic part of me off my back, and then moving on throughout my day. But that does little to help me grow closer to Jesus.

It's important to set time aside each day in order to have uninterrupted communication with the Lord. Of course, that communication is not just us talking to God but God talking to us. In order for us to clearly hear God's direction in our lives, it is necessary to shut the noise off and set aside a particular time each day with God to get alone with Him. You will be amazed at how much you grow closer to Jesus. You will discover that His Word is alive and active. It will penetrate your heart, break you where you need to be broken, lift you up when you are down, bring you encouragement for your soul and hope for your heart. Guard that time with God like you would guard an important appointment in your day.

Precious Savior, here's my plan for making regular time with You a priority. . . .

The Language of Worship

Who may worship in your sanctuary, LORD? Who may enter your presence on your holy hill? Those who lead blameless lives and do what is right, speaking the truth from sincere hearts. Those who refuse to gossip or harm their neighbors or speak evil of their friends.

PSALM 15:1–3

David tells us in Psalm 15:3 that in order to dwell on God's holy hill—in God's presence—we cannot be backbiters or slanderers with our words. In other words, we are never to circulate evil reports about others.

Have you ever been caught up in the crossfire of a vicious argument between two friends? And then they both pull you aside and want you to agree with them by slandering the other? I think we all end up in situations like that sometimes. But the Bible warns us to keep our mouths closed in these situations and to avoid doing harm to either side. It also goes on to warn us that we should not do any harm to anyone, especially those with whom we do business. Often we hear conversations around the church or in the office that eventually take us down a road of slander and even gossip. But remember, if our calling is to live a lifestyle of worship, we must steer clear of these things. Our speech should be marked by kindness, wisdom, and discretion.

O Lord, save me from the temptation of giving in to slander. Give me wisdom to walk with kindness and discretion.

How Do You Define the Word *Worship*?

Since you have been raised to new life with Christ, set your sights on the realities of heaven, where Christ sits in the place of honor at God's right hand. Think about the things of heaven, not the things of earth.

COLOSSIANS 3:1–2

When I was fresh out of college, I led several youth camps with Louis Giglio. During one of his talks, he gave a definition of worship that has stuck with me all these years. He said, "Worship is setting your mind's attention and your heart's affection on God . . . praising Him for who He is and what He's done."

That definition has always resonated with me because it reminds me that worship involves every part of us: our soul, mind, will, and body. It isn't just about gathering for church with other believers and singing praise songs once or twice a week. Worship is about who we are, not just what we are. And not only that, worship is about whose we are. We are God's children. He has given us life! Worship is the direct response of praise from our hearts straight to the heart of God. "The Lord is my strength and shield. I trust him with all my heart. He helps me, and my heart is filled with joy. I burst out in songs of thanksgiving" (Psalm 28:7).

Worship Him today for who He is and what He has done!

Thank You for making me Your child, heavenly Father. I praise You!

Worship in the Chaos

Search for the LORD and for his strength; continually seek him.

1 CHRONICLES 16:11

It's a crazy world, isn't it? The news is filled with everything from racial tensions in America to war in the Middle East to the ruthless killings of Christians in Iraq back to political maneuvering here in the States. All that plus the daily grind of just trying to survive another day of work, bill paying, e-mails, and carting our children around town.

So how do we keep the right focus on the right things amidst all this activity? There's only one way that I know of: We must spend enough time in the quiet presence of God.

How is your prayer life? I admit, mine has been quite poor at times. Most of us don't even spend three minutes a day in prayer. And yet that is where we find real peace from God in the middle of the chaos and hear His voice above the noise. I do believe our concept of prayer changes when we simply take enough time each day to contemplate the goodness of God and the sacrifice of His Son, Jesus. We will eventually be overcome by the power of His love and begin to delight in Him for who He is.

Learning to delight in God will bring us to another level of our worshiping lifestyle. Go to Him. Talk to Him. Listen to Him. Then trust Him.

In Your presence, dear Lord, is peace and fullness of joy. I seek You today!

What We See Greatly Affects Our Lifestyle of Worship

I will refuse to look at anything vile and vulgar. I hate all who deal crookedly; I will have nothing to do with them. I will reject perverse ideas and stay away from every evil.

PSALM 101:3–4

The eyes truly are the window to the soul. What we see and when we see it can change our lives forever. John Bunyan, who wrote *Pilgrim's Progress*, wrote another book called *The Holy War*. In it he taught that we have two main channels into our mind: what he called the Eye-gate and the Ear-gate. Through these two gates flow most of the knowledge we receive.

Today I want to talk about the Eye-gate. What we allow through that gate impacts our spirits more than we realize. Proverbs 4:25 tells us to "look straight ahead." And Proverbs 23:26 instructs: "My son, give me your heart. May your eyes take delight in following my ways." The connection between the heart and the eye is a clear one. Through the eyes flows knowledge to the heart.

What we let in through our Eye-gates affects our minds, and in turn our worship. We can't view trash and not expect it to touch our spirits. We must be diligent to guard our eyes to protect ourselves from sin so we can be free to worship with pure hearts.

Help me, Father, to guard my eyes, to honor You in everything I view.

A Balanced Life
Is an Act of Worship

*I have come down from heaven to do the will of God who sent me,
not to do my own will.*

JOHN 6:38

I'm constantly amazed at how Jesus kept such a healthy balance in His life. He was just never in a hurry. Always in control of His emotions, His actions, and His schedule.

One thing I've learned the hard way in my life is that if I don't keep a tight rein on my schedule, things can get out of line in a hurry. This causes me to get stressed, which causes me to get in a hurry, which causes me to make wrong decisions, and on it goes. Jesus lived with a stunning intentionality that was disciplined and driven by purpose. He was always cool, calm, and collected. Do you want to know why He was able to maintain balance? I firmly believe the reason is because He spent so much time in prayer with His heavenly Father.

Jesus told us that He came "to do the will of God who sent me, not to do my own will" (John 6:38) and "to seek and save those who are lost" (Luke 19:10). You want to live a balanced life? Let the intentional focus of Jesus inspire you. He communed with His Father, and He knew who He was, why He was here, and exactly where He was going.

Help me to follow Your example, Lord Jesus, of living a life of balance.

Worship in the Center of His Will

May the God of peace—who brought up from the dead our Lord Jesus, the great Shepherd of the sheep, and ratified an eternal covenant with his blood—may he equip you with all you need for doing his will. May he produce in you, through the power of Jesus Christ, every good thing that is pleasing to him. All glory to him forever and ever!

HEBREWS 13:20–21

Have you ever wondered whether you're living in the center of God's will? It can be difficult at times to discern exactly what His will is for us in certain situations, but one thing is for sure: It is His will, first and foremost, that you love Him with all your heart. This is the greatest commandment.

So the first step to living in the will of God is to fall in love with Jesus. This alone will prioritize your life and cause you to make wise decisions. Loving the Lord with all your heart will make you think before you act. Your heart's desire will be to please Him before any other. This in turn will open your ears to His voice. And when you're able to hear from God clearly, His will becomes a much clearer picture.

Jesus, may my love for You grow more and more each day so that it becomes my heart's desire to please You and obey Your will in all things.

Pure Worship
from a Pure Heart

Come close to God, and God will come close to you. Wash your hands, you sinners; purify your hearts, for your loyalty is divided between God and the world.

JAMES 4:8

Living the blessed life means we live a life of worship. And that is always a decision of the mind and an attitude of the heart. In the Bible, the "heart" is referred to as the inner part of one's being where choices are made and will is determined. So when Jesus says, "Blessed are the pure in heart . . . " (Matthew 5:8 NKJV), He is referring to those whose actions are untarnished by sin of any kind and whose will is bent toward pleasing God in all things.

There is only one Person who can give us a heart like that, and that is Jesus. Nothing short of a heart changed by Jesus will bring about a pure heart. Where is your heart today? Is it tainted by bad or selfish decisions you've made along the way? Is it clouded by selfishness and pride? Only you know. But I can promise you this: It is the pure in heart who will ultimately see God.

Let Jesus cleanse you today. We have His promise that "if we confess our sins to him, he is faithful and just to forgive us our sins and to cleanse us from all wickedness" (1 John 1:9).

Cleanse me today, Lord. I want to have a pure heart before You.

Stress with a Purpose

He knows where I am going. And when he tests me, I will come out as pure as gold.

JOB 23:10

Are you feeling stressed these days? When I watch the news, then couple that with the pressure of making sure I'm doing well in all my endeavors and being a good dad and husband, I can really get stressed out.

Stress is unavoidable. But it does have its benefits. It has a way of helping us differentiate between nonessentials and essentials. Stress helps us determine what is most important. And what is most important in our lives? Worship.

God purifies our hearts and our lives by putting us through the fires of stress. It is through this purifying process that we learn perseverance, or patience. Ultimately, through all of this, we are perfected in our faith. It is only those who have walked with the Lord a while, who have crawled through the depths of the valleys, who truly know what it is to worship the Lord with a perfected faith.

Yes, your stress and your trials do serve a purpose. That purpose is to draw you closer to the Lord and to learn how to strengthen your weak faith into a strong and unwavering walk with Jesus. Learn to worship God in the midst of the stress!

I acknowledge that in Your wisdom and love, Lord, You allow stress and trials in my life. Help me to worship You in the middle of the challenges.

Worship from the Shadows

Do not fear, for I am with you; do not be dismayed, for I am your God. I will strengthen you and help you; I will uphold you with my righteous right hand.

ISAIAH 41:10 NIV

When I was a young boy, I traveled with my family all over the western United States. My dad was an evangelist and we were in church nearly every night. One night we got to a church early and saw that there was a construction site on the premises. Large steel beams had been placed and the walls were framed, which cast looming shadows across the framing and floors as we walked the site. I must admit, I was scared of those shadows. So I leaned into my dad and said, "I hope a boogeyman doesn't come after us!" Then I added, "But I'm not scared because my daddy is with me." Those big shadows were scary, but in the shadow of my father, I felt secure.

In Psalm 17, we find David praying to God. He's afraid of his enemies, but then he makes this request: "Hide me under the shadow of Your wings" (17:8 NKJV). David recognized that even in the midst of stressful days and difficult situations, there was a shadow over him that shielded and protected. As worshipers of Jesus, always remember that we are under a bigger shadow: the shadow of His wings. Fear not. He will protect you. He will keep you.

When I'm afraid, God, I run to You and know that I am safe from all harm.

Worship God by Trusting Him

Trust in the LORD with all your heart; do not depend on your own understanding. Seek his will in all you do, and he will show you which path to take.

PROVERBS 3:5–6

Proverbs 3:5–6 is a wonderful admonition to trust in God through everything in our lives. Whether it be work or play, relationships or financial matters, we are to trust in the Lord with *all* our hearts. Of course, to trust in the Lord requires faith. It means completely relying on God's promises. It means we believe that His presence is not only with us but also that He will guide us.

We must come to the place in our walk with the Lord where we believe wholeheartedly that God is true to His Word, that He is able to handle any of our problems, and that He is wise enough to lead us in the right direction. If we want to learn to truly trust in Him, we must get intimately acquainted with His Word and His Spirit. It is in doing this that we find He wants to guide us in every area of our lives.

Our lifestyle of worship should be 24/7, 365 days a year. Begin even now to worship Him in all aspects of your life by simply acknowledging Him in all things. You already believe in Him as Savior. Now trust Him as guide.

I put my trust in You, my Savior and guide. You haven't failed me yet, and You never will.

Worship That Permeates

The word of God is alive and powerful. It is sharper than the sharpest two-edged sword, cutting between soul and spirit, between joint and marrow. It exposes our innermost thoughts and desires.

HEBREWS 4:12

The next time you're in church and everyone is singing a song, take a moment to look around. Ask yourself this question: *Do people really live what they are singing?* Then ask yourself the same question. You can't do anything about how others live, but you can do something about *your* walk with Christ.

Do you want to be a true worshiper of Jesus? Do you want to live what you sing about every Sunday? Then dive deep into His Word. Hebrews reminds us that His Word is living and active, and if we will allow it, it will penetrate our souls, which in turn will permeate our lives with the fragrance of Christ. In 2 Timothy we read, "All Scripture is given by inspiration of God, and is profitable for doctrine, for reproof, for correction, for instruction in righteousness, that the man of God may be complete, thoroughly equipped for every good work" (3:16–17 NKJV).

Do you want power in your walk with Christ? Infuse your life with the love of Christ. You will be surprised at how that will transform you from being one who just participates in worship services to one who is permeated by the power of Christ in your everyday living.

Lord, may Your love and power fill me and overflow from my life to those around me.

Worship That Imitates

Imitate God, therefore, in everything you do, because you are his dear children.

EPHESIANS 5:1

For years the phrase "What would Jesus do?" has been a popular saying among believers. WWJD. Everybody knows what it stands for. But the question is, do we really *know* what Jesus would do in any given situation? Have we studied His life and His Word enough to react as He would react, to say what He would say, and to love like He loves?

There is only one way to know what Jesus would do. We must spend time with Him and truly follow Him. We must read His Word and let His Spirit transform us.

Everything Jesus did when He was on earth was driven by love. In 1 John we are instructed, "Let us not love in word or in tongue, but in deed and in truth" (3:18 NKJV). In other words, if we want to be more like Jesus, then our love needs to be expressed in our words and in our actions.

Be imitators of God and "walk in love, as Christ also has loved us and given Himself for us, an offering and a sacrifice to God for a sweet-smelling aroma" (Ephesians 5:2 NKJV).

Lord, I want to follow in Your footsteps and love like You do. Help me to be faithful to get into Your Word and allow Your Spirit to make me more like You.

Worship That Irrigates

The rain and snow come down from the heavens and stay on the ground to water the earth. They cause the grain to grow, producing seed for the farmer and bread for the hungry. It is the same with my word. I send it out, and it always produces fruit. It will accomplish all I want it to, and it will prosper everywhere I send it.

ISAIAH 55:10–11

Many years ago farmers who lived in dry climates learned that they could not effectively grow crops if they relied completely on rainfall. Something had to be done to actively capture the rainwater and control the use of that water throughout the season. So they came up with the process of irrigation. Passively waiting on it to rain meant the loss of crops. Actively irrigating when it didn't rain created ways to sustain the crops.

And so it is with our lifestyle of worship. God has given us the power of His Spirit. He has already provided the rain. Now it is up to us to actively pursue growing in Him and living a lifestyle of worship and holiness. Just as the farmer uses what God has provided to grow his crops, so we must use what God has provided for us in His Spirit and His Word to actively grow in Him each and every day.

Thank You, Father, for providing everything I need to grow in You and live for You.

Worship That Fumigates

Our lives are a Christ-like fragrance rising up to God. But this fragrance is perceived differently by those who are being saved and by those who are perishing.

2 CORINTHIANS 2:15

I think we can all agree that body odor is a bad thing. That's why the shelves in department stores and drugstores are lined with deodorants, perfumes, colognes, and body sprays. We spend a great deal of money each year to make sure we smell good to others.

But what about our spirits? How do we smell spiritually?

Have you noticed how you can always spot the Christians who spend a lot of time with Jesus? There's a sweet fragrance that emanates from them because they've been in the presence of the Savior. They exude peace, and the love of Jesus is evident in their words and actions.

Paul refers to this as the fragrance of Christ in 2 Corinthians. We all emit a "scent" that either repels or attracts others. But for believers, our fragrance should be one that attracts others to Jesus. This sweet aroma breaks down the strongholds of pride and softens the hardest of hearts. It's the aroma of love. "By this all will know that you are My disciples, if you have love for one another" (John 13:35 NKJV).

Lord Jesus, may I be so filled with You as I spend time in Your presence that others can't help noticing the sweet fragrance of Jesus in my life.

Worship That Elevates

You have been called to live in freedom, my brothers and sisters. But don't use your freedom to satisfy your sinful nature. Instead, use your freedom to serve one another in love.

GALATIANS 5:13

Have you ever noticed how much easier it is to push somebody off a platform than it is to pull them up onto it?

Everyone has a testimony, and everyone has a reputation. That's why it's important for us to live as people with a strong set of values and principles and to most closely associate ourselves with people with strong character. Psalm 1 says, "Blessed is the man who walks not in the counsel of the ungodly, nor stands in the path of sinners" (1:1 NKJV). The happiest people on earth are those who wake up every morning rejoicing in the mercies of God and who go to bed every night with a clear conscience.

When you live a life that is free of addictions, free of immorality, and free from the trappings of sin, then you begin to understand the freedom that comes from knowing Christ. And when you hang around others who have experienced this kind of freedom, then your lifestyle of worship elevates those around you. So rather than pulling others down, you are lifting them up into a new level of worship.

Help me, Father, to walk in freedom so that I might lift others up by my example and by my words.

Individual Worship and Corporate Worship

The one thing I ask of the LORD—the thing I seek most—is to live in the house of the LORD all the days of my life, delighting in the LORD's perfections and meditating in his Temple.

PSALM 27:4

There are two kinds of worship: individual worship and corporate worship. One doesn't survive for long without the other. Individual worship is one-on-one time with the Lord. Corporate worship is gathering with other believers for the sake of meeting with God. The most powerful corporate worship happens when the room is filled with passionate individual worshipers. But more than that, corporate worship is that opportunity we have each week to fellowship with and encourage one another, to bear each other's burdens, and to gather together in unity at the foot of the cross with one heart, one mind, and one purpose.

Most believers go to church, but I'm not sure how many of us actually go with the purpose of worshiping God. This is due in large part to the fact that many who claim to know Christ have never really grown to worship Him on a daily basis. It's one thing to join a church, but it's another thing entirely to go to church as an individual worshiper of God. Do you want the Sunday church experience to change your life? Then start worshiping God as an individual today.

Lord, may I be a faithful worshiper of You both at home and at church.

Observing the Sabbath

Remember to observe the Sabbath day by keeping it holy. You have six days each week for your ordinary work, but the seventh day is a Sabbath day of rest dedicated to the LORD your God.

EXODUS 20:8–10

All of us would agree that it is good to practice the Ten Commandments. However, it's amazing how few of us actually practice the one God wrote the most about. We have no problem with "thou shalt not kill" and "thou shalt not steal," but what about the fact that He commands us to observe the Sabbath, a day of rest?

Maybe the world you live in doesn't allow time for you to stop, but God does. In fact, He commands it. I've had to learn this the hard way in my own life. As a high type-A personality and one who is driven to succeed, the thought of stopping to rest has always been a nuisance and seemed like a waste of time. But God matures us over time, and I have become wiser to the fact that my activity is much more productive when I am rested.

One of the great rewards in life is to stop working long enough to look back on what's been accomplished. I encourage you today to get serious about observing a Sabbath in your weekly rhythm. It will refocus you, refresh you, and replenish your worship of God.

Lord of the Sabbath, help me to be faithful to observe a day of rest as You ordained.

Ego-Driven Worship

He must become greater and greater, and I must become less and less.

JOHN 3:30

One of the dangers we all face in our walk with the Lord is this natural tendency to take credit for the things God does through us. So many times I've been leading worship with one hand in the air praising my Savior, but at the very same time internally patting myself on the back with the other hand for how good the band sounded or for singing the song so well.

I want to get to the point in my life where every moment of success or even failure is truly not about myself. I want to reach the point where the Spirit of God leads me through every moment of my day so that I am able to transform my life into a life that is completely surrendered to His thoughts and His ways. In other words, I pray for more humility. Not thinking less of myself, just thinking of myself less. I want to get to the place in my life where my sole desire is to be who God wants me to be, which then leads to doing what God wants me to do.

Let's focus on who we are becoming over and above what we are doing, and place ourselves in a position of humility before the Lord.

That's my desire Jesus. Help me to think of myself less and live to exalt You.

Worship in the Storms of Life

Those who live in the shelter of the Most High will find rest in the shadow of the Almighty. This I declare about the LORD: He alone is my refuge, my place of safety; he is my God, and I trust him.

PSALM 91:1–2

Remember the story of Peter walking on the water? Picture a terrifying storm out at sea. The disciples are working hard to keep their boat upright, and then they see what appears to be a ghost approaching them, walking on the water. The next thing we know, Peter is jumping out of the boat and beginning to walk on the water toward Jesus. But suddenly Peter begins to sink. Was it because the storm was so rough? I mean, everyone knows you can't walk on water during a storm, right? Oh wait, you can't walk on water when it's as calm as glass either!

The point is: It's not the storm that kept Peter from walking on water. He took his eyes off Jesus. His faith grew weak, and he began to sink. Please remember today, it's not the storms of life that keep us from becoming worshiping disciples of Jesus. It's only when we take our eyes off Him that we begin to falter. So turn your eyes back on Jesus today through any storm you may be facing!

My eyes are on You today, Lord Jesus. With You I'm safe in the storms!

Worship the Father as His Child

[Jesus] said, "I tell you the truth, unless you turn from your sins and become like little children, you will never get into the Kingdom of Heaven. So anyone who becomes as humble as this little child is the greatest in the Kingdom of Heaven."

MATTHEW 18:3–4

When children are afraid, in trouble, or hurt, their natural reaction is to run straight into the arms of Mom or Dad. The same goes for when they're happy and want to share their news. As a father, there is nothing more fulfilling than when one of my boys comes to me first with a need or a victory.

In Matthew 18, Jesus tells the disciples that we are to come to Him with the humility and guileless candor of a little child. And there, with arms wide open, He welcomes us as our loving Father. It reminds me of a song by Tommy Walker that I recorded a few years back: "Lord, I run to You. No one else will do. Lord, in troubled times, I will run straight to You; though my heart and flesh may fail, You're my ever-present help, my tower of strength, my portion evermore."

Our heavenly Father knows our needs, and we are held securely in His hands. As His children, one of the ways we worship Him is by seeking Him and praying to Him and asking Him to help us.

Father, I'm so grateful that I can run to You like a child and know You're there waiting with open arms!

The Worshiping Mentor

Work hard so you can present yourself to God and receive his approval. Be a good worker, one who does not need to be ashamed and who correctly explains the word of truth.

2 TIMOTHY 2:15

One of the most wonderful things about Jesus is the fact that He didn't lead His disciples from a distance. He didn't camp out in Nazareth and send them messages on where to go and what to do. He was down in the trenches with them. He was walking with them and talking with them each and every day. Most of all, He was showing them how to live and how to think. Those three years were a lab, not a classroom. As a result, the world was changed forever.

His is a beautiful example for us to follow as we lead those in our sphere of influence. Every one of us is in a role of leadership in some way. We lead others by influencing them. We influence others by teaching them. We teach others by showing them and inspiring them. We inspire others by building them up and serving them. And in turn, by serving them, we end up influencing them again.

So use the model Jesus gave us. Let your walk match your talk and show the people in your life what a lifestyle of worship looks like.

Please help me, Lord, to lead others by example and always be willing to get down in the trenches with them.

Perverted Worship

The temptations in your life are no different from what others experience. And God is faithful. He will not allow the temptation to be more than you can stand. When you are tempted, he will show you a way out so that you can endure. So, my dear friends, flee from the worship of idols.

1 CORINTHIANS 10:13–14

Bad habits are hard to conquer. Some habits can lead to addiction. Addictions eventually will lead to our downfall and some can even cause death. Addiction has been called "misplaced worship," which leads to idolatry. Misplaced worship means that we have chosen and become totally consumed by someone or something other than our relationship with the Lord Jesus. This usually happens slowly and subtly.

Many people who fall prey to addictions still believe they can replace that bad habit with a good one. But good habits don't fix bad habits. They typically just add on to it. We were created to worship, so we'll always seek to worship something. Is there anything enslaving you today? What in your life is more important than your growing relationship with Jesus? Do you have an addiction that is hindering you? Moral reformation without spiritual regeneration never leads to total transformation. We must surrender ourselves to the pure worship of the Lord. The only way to do so is to allow Jesus to cleanse us from any and all addictions that hinder our walk with Him.

Lord, may I be able to truthfully say that nothing is more important to me than my relationship with You!

Be a Witnessing Worshiper

Give thanks to the Lord and proclaim his greatness. Let the whole world know what he has done. Sing to him; yes, sing his praises. Tell everyone about his wonderful deeds.

PSALM 105:1–2

Psalm 105 is a wonderful psalm of praise to the Lord. In it, the writer encourages us to sing to the Lord. But he also tells us to talk to others about His wondrous works. How often do you do that?

You know, the true worshiping servant of God is one who has a growing and intimate relationship with his or her Savior. How many deep relationships have you ever been involved in where you never spoke about that person to anyone? None, right? When you love someone, you talk about them openly and proudly. You tell of the qualities you like about them, things they did with you, things they said to you.

Life with someone you deeply love is exciting and full of adventure. And so it should be in our relationship with Jesus. When we are consumed with our relationship with Jesus, we end up witnessing for Him. Not in a forced sort of way, but rather as the natural outflow of a lifestyle of loving Him. Whom can you share your love for Jesus with today?

I want to shout it from the rooftops, Lord: I love Jesus and He loves me! Help me to boldly share Your love today. Show me who needs a touch from You.

The Mighty Voice of the Lord

Listen carefully to the thunder of God's voice as it rolls from his mouth. It rolls across the heavens, and his lightning flashes in every direction. Then comes the roaring of the thunder—the tremendous voice of his majesty. He does not restrain it when he speaks. God's voice is glorious in the thunder. We can't even imagine the greatness of his power.

JOB 37:2–5

I love Psalm 29. It's a psalm of David, and it's all about the voice of the Lord. "The voice of the LORD is over the waters. The God of glory thunders. . . . The voice of the LORD is powerful; the voice of the LORD is full of majesty. The voice of the LORD breaks the cedars. . . . The voice of the LORD divides the flames of fire. The voice of the LORD shakes the wilderness" (Psalm 29:3–5, 7–8 NKJV).

God's presence is everywhere. His power is unmatched. His might is undeniable. And His voice is recognizable. Sometimes He speaks to us through the still, small voice of His Holy Spirit. But have you ever considered the fact that God's voice is shouting throughout all creation as well? There's no doubt about it: The voice of the Lord is active and mighty.

The question is: As His worshiping servant, how long has it been since you took the time to listen?

Your voice is mighty, O God, and yet tender. How good You are! I tune my heart today to hear Your voice whispering to me.

Worship Him in Peace

The faithful love of the LORD never ends! His mercies never cease. Great is his faithfulness; his mercies begin afresh each morning.

LAMENTATION 3:22–23

Several years ago, my wife and I took a trip in the early fall to Cape Cod. We stayed in a beautiful hotel right at the turn of the cape in Chatham, Massachusetts. One early morning, I got up and went out to the front porch of the hotel, which was lined with rocking chairs. I was able to sit and watch the sun rise over the horizon of the ocean. It was a glorious sight!

I'll never forget the overwhelming sense of peace that flooded my soul that morning. It was a tremendous reminder of the fact that God's mercies are new each and every day. And the mercies I experience today are completely different from the mercies waiting on me tomorrow. Just knowing that gives me peace to move throughout this day with confidence and assurance.

In John 16:33, Jesus reminds us that in this world we will have many trials and sorrows, but we can take heart because He has overcome the world. "I have told you all this so that you may have peace in me."

So be of good cheer. Let His peace reign in your heart, knowing that He holds your day in His hands.

Today I embrace the peace that's mine in Christ, Lord Jesus. Let it rule and reign in my heart.

Are You Hungry for Worship?

I lift my hands to you in prayer. I thirst for you as parched land thirsts for rain.

PSALM 143:6

When my son Cooper was younger, we had a hard time getting him to eat his food during meals. On one occasion, we couldn't get him to eat even three bites of his lunch. We grew very frustrated with him, so after quite a bit of negotiating, I had had enough. I told him he would have to sit at that table until he ate at least half his lunch. Would you believe that at five that afternoon, he still hadn't eaten? It was a Sunday, and time for us to go back to church, so I finally gave in.

Later that night, I thought about the whole scenario and this simple thought entered my head: Cooper wouldn't eat his lunch because he wasn't hungry enough. Yes, he was being stubborn and testing his boundaries as a child, but had he been starving, there's no doubt he would gladly have eaten. Could it be that the reason we don't worship the Lord like we should is simply because we aren't hungry enough for His presence in our lives? In Matthew 5:6, Jesus says, "Blessed are those who hunger and thirst for righteousness, for they shall be filled" (NKJV). This verse isn't just about basic needs, but about passion. How long has it been since your primary passion in life was following Jesus?

Jesus, increase my hunger for You!

Good Worship
and Bad Worship

Christ's love controls us. Since we believe that Christ died for all, we also believe that we have all died to our old life. He died for everyone so that those who receive his new life will no longer live for themselves. Instead, they will live for Christ, who died and was raised for them.

2 CORINTHIANS 5:14–15

I can't tell you how many times people have come up to me after a worship service I've led and said something like, "That was good worship today." Of course, many times that simply means, "Hey, I like those songs." And therefore, bad worship would mean they don't like the songs, right?

Remember, true worship is really not about a song at all. True worship is a lifestyle that honors God in all things. True worship is not about a where or a when, but rather about a who and a how! Jesus addressed this issue with the Samaritan woman at the well when He said, "True worshipers will worship the Father in spirit and in truth" (John 4:23). And through a powerful conversation, Jesus helped her understand that the quality of worship is our true measure of devotion to God.

So what is good worship? A life fully devoted to Christ. What is bad worship? A life fully devoted to self.

My life is Yours, Lord. Help me to live fully devoted to You.

A Lesson from the Sparrow

Don't worry about anything; instead, pray about everything. Tell God what you need, and thank him for all he has done.

PHILIPPIANS 4:6

It was my senior year at Samford University. One weekend, I was leading worship for a little Methodist retreat center in Cook Springs, Alabama. I was stressed from taking twenty-one hours in one semester, trying to graduate, and starting my new ministry, and I couldn't sleep. So I got up early that Saturday morning to read my Bible before the last session started. I began reading out of Matthew 10, where Jesus says, "What is the price of two sparrows—one copper coin? But not a single sparrow can fall to the ground without your Father knowing it. And the very hairs on your head are all numbered. So don't be afraid; you are more valuable to God than a whole flock of sparrows" (Matthew 10:29–31).

After I finished reading this passage, I wrote a poem which later became my first song which God then used to begin my ministry three months later.

If you're worried today, hold on and wait. God has you. He's got whatever burden you're carrying. Trust Him with it. If He cares for even the smallest of birds, will He not care for you as His own children?

I bring my troubles to You, strong Father. Nothing is too difficult for You—even this thing. I trust Your plan for my life.

Honor God with Your Relationships

Always be humble and gentle. Be patient with each other, making allowance for each other's faults because of your love. Make every effort to keep yourselves united in the Spirit, binding yourselves together with peace.

EPHESIANS 4:2–3

I'll be honest. I've never been the best at relationships. Getting into the real lives of others and letting them into my life can get messy and complicated. And yet, when we look at the life of Jesus, we see that that's exactly what He did, especially with His twelve disciples. Those guys were together 24/7 for three and a half years. Do you think they got to know each other pretty well? Here was God Himself, in the flesh, eating, sharing with, sleeping, and working right alongside a bunch of ragtag misfits just like you and me. And yet, through it all, He showed us how to live. He showed us how to build relationships.

Jesus first honored His Father in all things. That's worship. But second to that came His relationships with people. Honor God today by diving into the lives of others. Don't be afraid to get your hands dirty. When you invest your time, your resources, and your energy into others, you end up getting blessed yourself.

Lord, help me to be always ready to pour myself out to bless others and show them Your love. May I never be afraid to get my hands dirty.

Love Is Spelled T-I-M-E

Is there any encouragement from belonging to Christ? Any comfort from his love? Any fellowship together in the Spirit? Are your hearts tender and compassionate? Then make me truly happy by agreeing wholeheartedly with each other, loving one another, and working together with one mind and purpose.

PHILIPPIANS 2:1–2

One thing I've learned as a husband and father is that no amount of words can replace just being there for your loved ones. I had to learn this the hard way, when I was on the road for over 230 nights a year at one point and was constantly away from home. My life was completely out of balance because I was totally consumed with building a career and was missing out on the chance to build my family. And my family suffered because they just wanted me to *be there.*

Well, God broke me of that and things are much better now, but I still struggle to find balance because building a family, or any relationship, requires a tremendous amount of quality time. "Redeem the time," the Bible tells us (NKJV). And you know what I'm learning? To redeem the time doesn't always mean we make ourselves busier. It doesn't always mean we need to be in a hurry. Sometimes it means that we just sit— and listen, and learn, and love.

I pray for Your help, Father, to be generous with my time with my loved ones.

From Mourning to Worshiping

I turned to the Lord God and pleaded with him in prayer and fasting. I also wore rough burlap and sprinkled myself with ashes. . . . But the Lord our God is merciful and forgiving, even though we have rebelled against him.

DANIEL 9:3, 9

Everyone faces difficult times and every one of us will experience times of mourning at some point in our lives. Usually these times come when we lose a loved one or go through a severe crisis.

Nobody enjoys mourning, and yet Jesus told us, "Blessed are those who mourn, for they shall be comforted" (Matthew 5:4 NKJV). What did He mean by that? This mourning that Jesus referred to is not just about mourning over a loss or a tragedy; He was also talking about mourning over a sin-filled and lost world. It is in this mourning that we open our heavy hearts to the Lord and we discover that our grieving is not without hope. There is still time for change. Peace can still rule and reign in the hearts of countless souls if revival comes.

Let your heart break over the condition of this world, but always remember, you are on the winning side. So stand strong, pray hard, and worship loud!

O Jesus, break my heart for what breaks Yours! May revival sweep this land and hearts be turned to the only One who can make them whole.

Live a Life of Discretion

Discretion is a life-giving fountain to those who possess it, but discipline is wasted on fools.

PROVERBS 16:22

One of the keys to preserving relationships and reputations is to practice discretion in our daily living. What exactly is discretion? Merriam-webster.com defines it this way: "the quality of being careful about what you do and say so that people will not be embarrassed or offended: the quality of being discreet." When things happen to us that make us want to react harshly and say or do things we'll regret, discretion is having the discipline to keep our mouths shut and our actions in line. When someone shares personal information with us in confidence, discretion is keeping that information to ourselves in order to protect them.

People who are filled with the wisdom of God have discretion. Listen to what Proverbs 2 says: "When wisdom enters your heart, and knowledge is pleasant to your soul, discretion will preserve you; understanding will keep you" (2:10–11 NKJV). And the more we practice discretion in our lives, the less appealing sin will be to us. We will find that we refrain from saying things we shouldn't. We will find that we refuse to do things that will cause others to stumble or be hurt. And we discover that what we wear and where we go will be motivated by our love for Jesus.

Lord, may Your wisdom guide my life; may all my words and actions be ruled by discretion.

How Great Is Our God!

No eye has seen, no ear has heard, and no mind has imagined what God has prepared for those who love him.

1 CORINTHIANS 2:9

The story goes that one morning a young boy approached his father and asked him, "What does heaven look like?" His father responded and said: "This afternoon while you are under the deck playing with your trucks, look up and see what is underneath that floorboard." So the young boy did what his father asked. But when he looked up, he saw nothing but dirt dauber nests, spiderwebs, and ugliness.

That evening when his father returned from work, the boy told him he had done just as his father had told him, but he didn't understand. His father told him he would give him the answer after dinner. So after dinner, when the sun had set and the sky was lit with stars, the father took his son outside and stood still beneath the gorgeous moonlit night. Then he said, "Remember how I told you to look up while you were underneath that deck and see what lies beneath the floorboard? I want you to look up now. You see how beautiful that night sky is? I can't tell you what heaven looks like, but that, my son, is just the floorboard."

God in heaven, thank You that You are preparing a place for me now that is more beautiful than anything I will ever see here on earth!

Praying Through the Pain

The Spirit of the Sovereign LORD is upon me, for the LORD has anointed me to . . . comfort the brokenhearted.

ISAIAH 61:1

Pain can come in a variety of forms. There is physical pain, of course, but also the pain that comes from losing a loved one, the pain of loneliness, the pain of a broken relationship, the pain of hurt feelings, and the list goes on. Whatever it may be, chances are you've experienced real pain in your life. Sometimes it's not easy to get past it. But it's good to remember today that God is our refuge. We worship the One who "heals the brokenhearted and binds up their wounds" (Psalm 147:3 NKJV). He is "close to the brokenhearted; he rescues those whose spirits are crushed" (Psalm 34:18). And the best news of all: There is coming a day when God will ultimately take all His children from the pains of this earth and "will wipe every tear from their eyes, and there will be no more death or sorrow or crying or pain. All these things are gone forever" (Revelation 21:4).

Go to the Lord with your pain. Bow before Him and worship Him. He knows your situation, He understands your emotions, and He hears your cries.

Father, thank You that You understand my pain. I bring it before You today. Please heal the broken places!

Let God Change Your Taste Buds

Take delight in the LORD, and he will give you your heart's desires.

PSALM 37:4

I meet new Christians all the time who have come out of intensely immoral backgrounds, or who have been rescued out of horribly abusive situations or who have been set free from the bondage of addiction. In every case, the grace of God has done something radical: It has changed their taste buds. No longer is there an appetite for the sinful things they used to do in the past. Instead, they are hungry for the Word of God and thirsty for righteousness. They have found peace, comfort, and joy in the presence of God. They have been set free by the blood of Jesus!

You see, the blessed life is the life that delights in the Word of God and the things of God. "Oh, the joys of those who do not follow the advice of the wicked, or stand around with sinners, or join in with mockers. But they delight in the law of the Lord, meditating on it day and night" (Psalm 1:1–2).

How's your appetite? Have you allowed God to change your taste buds? Are you hungry for more of Him? "Taste and see that the Lord is good. Oh, the joys of those who take refuge in him!" (Psalm 34:8).

Lord, increase my appetite for more of You, and may my taste buds reflect the changes You've made in me.

Let Your Worship Revolve Around the Son

O LORD, I will honor and praise your name, for you are my God. You do such wonderful things! You planned them long ago, and now you have accomplished them.

ISAIAH 25:1

I read an article the other day about how chaotic our universe would be if the planets of our solar system didn't revolve around the sun. We certainly wouldn't be alive long or even have a chance at sustained life. But because the earth revolves around the sun at just the right speed and just the right distance, we don't freeze or burn up, we enjoy seasons, and we have just the right amount of oxygen.

Did you know that over 25 percent of the American population believes the sun revolves around the earth? Crazy, right? Now, what does that have to do with worship? Well, our worship should revolve around another Son—not S-U-N, but S-O-N, the living Son of God. And just as the earth can't survive long without revolving around the burning sun, we won't be able to sustain a solid Christian life without staying close to Jesus, the risen Son. So let everything in your life revolve around Jesus. He never moves. He never changes. Draw near to Him today.

Lord Jesus, let me never forget that it's all about You. You are my Sustainer and my Light.

Worship Around the World

After this I saw a vast crowd, too great to count, from every nation and tribe and people and language, standing in front of the throne and before the Lamb. They were clothed in white robes and held palm branches in their hands.

REVELATION 7:9

'll never forget the moment when I was asked to step to the front of St. Anne's Cathedral in Jerusalem and sing "The Lord's Prayer." When I started singing, it was as if the entire place knew I was singing a prayer, so the few hundred people milling about the cathedral stopped walking and waited for me to finish. A holy hush filled the room as I sang the last note. Then, off to my right, a man from another country stepped onto the stair beside me, to my surprise, and began to sing "I Need Thee Every Hour" in his own language. To my astonishment, when he got to the chorus, all the people in the room began to sing it in their own language. It was a holy moment for sure, and it reminded me of the universal power of the good news of God's grace. No matter who we are or where we are from, we all need the love of Jesus.

Let that truth sink deep into your heart and impact your worship.

Thank You, Jesus, that the Good News is for everyone. May that truth impact how I treat others.

Worship with Boldness

Paul . . . welcomed all who visited him, boldly proclaiming the Kingdom of God and teaching about the Lord Jesus Christ.

ACTS 28:30–31

We live in interesting times. These are days in which tolerance is preached boldly—until you preach Jesus boldly. Then the tolerant aren't so tolerant anymore. These are days when acceptance is touted as a must in our society—until you stand boldly for Jesus. Then you aren't so accepted anymore.

We must remember that the very nature of the gospel of the Lord Jesus is offensive to all those who don't believe. So we must serve and present the Word of God to the unbeliever with love and a lifestyle that is consistent and holy, but still unashamed. When we live boldly for Christ and display our faith publicly, people will clearly see it. Our neighbors, coworkers, friends, and family will have no doubt as to where our hearts belong. It doesn't mean we're obnoxious or rude or arrogant. Rather, we will be known by our love.

But don't be surprised when ridicule comes. Jesus told us to expect it. Don't be surprised when it seems like every religion or agenda is favored above that of the Christian church. Jesus warned us about that. Instead, stay faithful. Worship boldly. Love loudly. And live honestly. God will honor you for that, and you will see many lives changed along the way.

Lord, may I never be afraid to stand boldly for You!

Worship Jesus, the Everlasting Savior

Are You not from everlasting, O LORD my God, my Holy One?

HABAKKUK 1:12 NKJV

Jesus wasn't just a temporary being. True, He dwelt among us only for a short while, but He has always been. He was there before creation, and He will be there throughout eternity. In plain old Virginian English, He ain't goin' nowhere! He was, is, and always will be. Jesus just *is*! He is the Alpha and Omega. The Beginning and the End. The same yesterday, today, and forever! His beginning wasn't the manger, and His ending wasn't the cross. Are you getting the picture?

The word *everlasting* reminds me that Jesus has always been and will always be King of kings and Lord of lords. He was never created; He is the Creator! He will never die; He conquered death! He didn't just walk the earth and go away. His presence and reign will never end. Our relationship with Him cannot be undone. Our hope is permanently sealed by His grace. He will never stop loving us. Nothing can take us out of His hand.

Doesn't it comfort you to know that we worship a Savior who is everlasting? He will never leave us nor forsake us. He is going to be there through it all!

Everlasting Savior, thank You that You are always the same, that You never change. You are my rock and my fortress.

Solitary Worship

Jesus often withdrew to the wilderness for prayer.

LUKE 5:16

Right before Jesus fed the five thousand in the miracle of the loaves and fishes, He received news that His cousin and friend John the Baptist had been beheaded by King Herod. Great crowds had been following Jesus everywhere He went, but when He heard this tragic news, Jesus responded by withdrawing from the crowd to be by Himself. "As soon as Jesus heard the news, he left in a boat to a remote area to be alone"(Matthew 14:13). He needed to commune with His Father in solitude, to collect His thoughts and process all that had just transpired.

Throughout our lives we will receive discouraging news and go through difficult times. It's not a matter of if but when. The real question is, what will we do when those times come? What can we learn from Jesus's example? We learn that the first thing we should do is get alone with God. Find a quiet place to pour out our souls to Him in prayer. Allow His Spirit to be our first and greatest comforter. Allow His Word to penetrate our hearts and minds before anything else.

If you're going through a difficult time today, I encourage you to follow the example of Christ: Go to a place by yourself and let Him minister to you.

Lord, I want to follow Your example. When tough times hit, may my first response be to come running to You before anyone or anything else.

Words of Life

Some people make cutting remarks, but the words of the wise bring healing.

PROVERBS 12:18

In James 3 we are told, "No man can tame the tongue. It is an unruly evil, full of deadly poison. With it we bless our God and Father, and with it we curse men, who have been made in the similitude of God. Out of the same mouth proceed blessing and cursing" (3:8–10 NKJV).

Isn't it amazing how much power the tongue has? It has the power to bring peace or to start a war. So much hinges on what we say and how we say it.

As worshipers of the Most High God, we have the opportunity each and every day to offer up words of life and encouragement to those around us. We must consciously make the choice to speak in a language of love and bless those with whom we work. It's important that those around us hear words of love from our hearts and then see loving actions that match those words.

That little muscle in our mouth has great power to either bless or curse. I want to encourage you, as part of your lifestyle of worship, to be very careful how you use your tongue, to think before you speak. Remember, your worship is a lifestyle of consistently speaking words of blessing and life.

Put a guard over my tongue, Lord, so I speak only words that give life and lift up those around me.

Loaves and Fishes

Jesus took the five loaves and two fish, looked up toward heaven, and blessed them. Then, breaking the loaves into pieces, he gave the bread to the disciples, who distributed it to the people. They all ate as much as they wanted, and afterward, the disciples picked up twelve baskets of leftovers. About 5,000 men were fed that day, in addition to all the women and children!

MATTHEW 14:19–21

Matthew 14 records one of the greatest miracles of all time. Jesus, having just received word of the death of His cousin and confidant John the Baptist, is emotionally drained and physically tired. Yet there is a massive crowd following Him and He is moved with compassion for them because they are as "sheep without a shepherd" (Matthew 9:36). He saw their spiritual needs, but He also saw their physical needs. They were not only spiritually starving, they were physically hungry too.

The disciples tried to get Jesus to disperse the crowd, but Jesus didn't want to let go of this opportunity to minister. So, as only He can do, He took five loaves and two fish offered by a boy and turned it into a feast with plenty of leftovers.

There is so much to learn here, but let's start with this one principle: God is the only One who can fill your life with all that you need.

It's true, Lord. I'm learning that when my soul is hungry, only You satisfy. To Your name be all the glory!

The Ultimate Act of Worship

Look after each other so that none of you fails to receive the grace of God. Watch out that no poisonous root of bitterness grows up to trouble you, corrupting many.

HEBREWS 12:15

All of us have been wronged at some point by someone. If you haven't, hang on—it'll happen! So when it does, the question is how we will handle it.

Jesus reminds us in His Sermon on the Mount to "turn the other cheek" when others wrong us. In other words, forgive. We should respond to others with grace and personally get better from the experience. If we choose to respond to the situation with anger, we will eventually become bitter.

I truly believe that one reason we have so many unhappy Christians in our churches is because so many of us have allowed the seeds of bitterness to take root in our hearts. Unfortunately, those roots, if they aren't dealt with, will deepen and infiltrate every area of our lives.

To live a life with an unforgiving heart doesn't just damage your relationships with others, it damages your own soul. You will look up one day and realize your heart of worship has been covered in a dark cloud of bitterness. Ask yourself as a worshiper today: Have I truly forgiven others? Or am I holding a grudge and allowing bitterness to set in?

Lord, reveal any bitterness that I've allowed to take root and heal me. May I always be quick to forgive.

Yes and No Worshipers

Speak the truth in love, growing in every way more and more like Christ, who is the head of his body, the church.

EPHESIANS 4:15

One of the reasons I was attracted to Shae, my wife, is because of her honesty. When we were dating, if I asked her which restaurant she wanted to go to, she would actually tell me! I never have to question what she thinks. She is honest and straightforward. I like that, because it takes all the guesswork out of our relationship. I know where she stands.

In His Sermon on the Mount, Jesus tells us to be this way. He warns us not to get caught up in swearing an oath to someone. And then He tells us to "let your 'Yes' be 'Yes,' and your 'No,' 'No'" (Matthew 5:37 NKJV). In other words, people should never have to guess where we stand. Our level of character as worshipers should be such that we don't have to add any other assurances to our words. We must be honest with one another and treat each other justly.

Today, as an act of worship, don't avoid it, but rather speak the truth in love to someone. Your honest candor might actually be quite refreshing to them. As you live a life of worship today, be honest in your conversations.

Help me, Father, to be honest in all my conversations today, to speak the truth in love.

Worshiping the Lord in the Light

If we are living in the light, as God is in the light, then we have fellowship with each other, and the blood of Jesus, his Son, cleanses us from all sin.

1 JOHN 1:7

Jesus not only loves us, He likes us too! He really wants to be with us and fellowship with us on a daily basis.

But what if we go to church with people we don't like? Or work next to someone we don't care for? What if our neighbor is the last person on earth we would actually hang out with? How do we worship the Lord around people like that? The answer: We must walk in the light of Jesus. "If we walk in the light as He is in the light, we have fellowship with one another" (1 John 1:7 NKJV). This means that if our relationship with Jesus is growing and strong, then we are able to at least be around those we have no affection for and live peaceably. So don't allow your dislike of another to hinder your worship. And certainly don't let bitterness toward another hinder it either. Ask God to help you see them through His eyes. Learn to enjoy and walk in the light of Jesus.

Worship begins with humility and servitude. Jesus lived each and every day with this spirit of love. As worshipers, may we strive to do the same!

Help me to view others through eyes of love, Father, and not let my personal preferences hinder my worship.

The Apple of His Eye

Keep me as the apple of your eye; hide me in the shadow of your wings.

PSALM 17:8 NIV

In Psalm 17, David asks the Lord to keep him as the apple of His eye. The "apple of the eye" refers to the pupil. As you know, our eyes are fragile but incredibly valuable. God created our faces in such a way that our eyes are protected and surrounded by bone.

So when David asks God to keep him as the "apple of His eye," he is essentially saying, "Lord, keep me in this place of protection. I am weak. I am vulnerable. I need to know I am in a secure position held by Your strength. And keep me there. Don't let me go."

Does that sound like a prayer you might have made at some point in your life? The reality is, every day you and I step out into an unknown world of potential trouble, tragedy, and temptation. So it's comforting to know that we are held securely in His hands. He will not let us go, and His Word promises that nothing can pluck us out of His hands. We are His children. We are His loved ones, truly the apple of His eye. "Many are the afflictions of the righteous, but the Lord delivers him out of them all" (Psalm 34:19 NKJV).

How blessed I am, gracious Father, to be the apple of Your eye! What safety, what security, what peace is mine!

Has God Given You a Vision?

Where there is no vision, the people are unrestrained, but happy is he who keeps the law.

PROVERBS 29:18 NASB

Helen Keller once said, "It's a terrible thing to see and have no vision." What exactly is vision? Vision is hope that is clearly defined. Vision is what sets the direction for your life. It is the motivator that moves you from simply existing to really living. It enables you to keep moving forward.

Every business owner knows that in order to succeed, he must have a vision and he must have a plan. But have you considered that in order to grow spiritually, you also need a vision and a plan? Without them you won't get very far. So what is your plan for spiritual growth? What is your vision for growing closer to the Lord in the coming months? What is your worship blueprint, if you will?

Growing into a mature worshiper takes time, discipline, determination, and desire. It won't be the easiest journey, but I can promise you this: it is certainly the most rewarding. Seek the Lord today and ask Him to give you vision for this year.

Lord, what is Your vision for my life? Show me what plans I need to make to keep growing spiritually. Save me from giving in to inertia and just drifting.

Lord, Please Bless This Day

This is the day the LORD has made. We will rejoice and be glad in it. Please, LORD, please save us. Please, LORD, please give us success.

PSALM 118:24–25

Each morning when I wake up I look to the ceiling and say these same words to God: "Lord, please bless this day." It's an important way for me to start the day because by doing that, I'm acknowledging that this is the day the Lord has made. I'm confessing to Him that I'm in need of His help to carry me through it, and that I'm looking forward to what He will do to use me in it. It reminds me that His mercies are new every morning, and that the blessings and mercies of yesterday are not the same as those I will encounter on this day.

I just love the fact that every morning is a fresh start with God, with our relationships with others, and with ourselves! I encourage you to take advantage of the opportunities the Lord has given you this day. This is the day that the Lord has made, so I lift my hands and give Him praise. I know He's watching over me—and He's watching over you.

Thank You, heavenly Father, for this fresh, new day and for Your fresh mercies. Please bless this day and fill it with opportunities to worship and serve You!

The Fruits of Worship

You can identify them by their fruit, that is, by the way they act.

MATTHEW 7:16

I love fruit. My favorite is watermelon. But watermelon doesn't grow on trees. So I'm pretty sure Jesus wasn't talking about watermelon when He said, "Every good tree bears good fruit, but a bad tree bears bad fruit" (Matthew 7:17 NKJV). Nevertheless, He was talking about the difference between a believer who glorifies God and lives for Him in all things and a person who doesn't worship God as a lifestyle and shows no evidence of faith in their lives.

It's a simple formula. Those who know and love Christ will produce fruit in their lives that represent the character of Christ: love, joy, peace, patience, goodness, kindness, faithfulness, gentleness, and self-control. And the very first fruit on that list is love. There isn't a more obvious clue to the world that you are a Christ-follower than when you genuinely love others. Love is the greatest of all virtues. It is love that motivates us to serve. It is love that moves us to respond to someone's needs with no expectation of reward. Love overcomes all barriers, speaks in every language, and shares the truth of the gospel of Jesus with more clarity than even the greatest of orators.

So worship God by loving Him first, and then truly and humbly loving others. As a worshiper, do others know you by these fruits?

Master Gardener, work in my life so that the fruit of the Spirit might be evident—especially love!

Do You Practice Social Holiness?

Let us cleanse ourselves from everything that can defile our body or spirit. And let us work toward complete holiness because we fear God.

2 CORINTHIANS 7:1

Holiness is often viewed as a very personal lifestyle, a discipline that is privately practiced. But true holiness doesn't stop with our own condition. It should carry out into our everyday actions that affect the world around us. You can't live a holy life privately and have it not show publicly. It's impossible. Why? Because if you're pursuing holiness in your life, it comes out in what you do, not just in who you are.

Let's keep in mind today that our lifestyle of worship demands that we strive to live lives that are fully committed to Him—not just in the church building, but in the office, in our homes, in our neighborhoods, and everywhere else we are. Can you imagine what our world would be like if every Christian passionately pursued holiness? How would the pursuit of holiness affect our daily decisions? What kinds of things would we give up? What sort of things would we start doing? Or what would we stop doing?

Imagine where your walk with Christ would be after five consistent years of passionately following Him and seeking daily to live a holy lifestyle. May we never forget that our mission is to make God's invisible kingdom visible in every aspect of our lives.

Light a fire under me, gracious God, to passionately pursue a holy lifestyle that honors Your name.

Hunting for Wisdom

Tune your ears to wisdom, and concentrate on understanding. Cry out for insight, and ask for understanding. Search for them as you would for silver; seek them like hidden treasures. Then you will understand what it means to fear the Lord, and you will gain knowledge of God.

PROVERBS 2:2–5

I'm clueless about hunting. In fact, when I was in junior high, my friends talked me into going snipe hunting during summer camp. As I tramped through the woods with a paper bag and a stick, my friends made their way back to the cabin for a good long laugh. I had no idea there was no such thing as a snipe. So after a very long search, I realized I was hunting for something that simply didn't exist.

Hunting for something that isn't real can be defeating. But hunting for something valuable and truly finding it can be incredibly rewarding. That's the way it is with God's wisdom. In order to live more fulfilled lives that are increasing in favor with God and mankind, we need more wisdom. The best place to hunt for wisdom is in the wisdom writings of Solomon, the wisest man to ever live. The book of Proverbs is my favorite of the wisdom writings because each verse is like a one-sentence, power-packed sermon about how we can get along better with others and with God. As worshipers, let's hunt for wisdom.

Today, God, I'm going hunting for wisdom in that wisest of books, Proverbs. May the treasures I find transform my heart and mind.

What Is Idol Worship?

You must not make for yourself an idol of any kind or an image of anything in the heavens or on the earth or in the sea. You must not bow down to them or worship them, for I, the Lord your God, am a jealous God.

EXODUS 20:4–5

All throughout Scripture we see that idol worship was a very common thing. Most of the time when we think of idol worship, we think of a golden calf or a statue of Baal. We tend to think of physical objects from an ancient time practiced by ancient cultures. But idol worship is still very much alive today. It may not come in the form of a golden calf, but instead in the form of a physical possession, a hobby or a habit, or even a relationship.

We must be careful that nothing takes precedence over our relationship with Christ and our love for Him. This is one mark of a true worshiper. Worship is a lifestyle, so I must keep my wants and my desires and my passions in check so that I don't allow other things in my life to take over my love for Christ and become an idol.

Lord Jesus, I confess that I have allowed _____ to become an idol in my life. With Your help, I tear it down and put You back on the throne of my heart, which is Your rightful place.

Righteous Thinking Leads to Righteous Living

The weapons of our warfare are not carnal but mighty in God for pulling down strongholds . . . bringing every thought into captivity to the obedience of Christ.

2 CORINTHIANS 10:4–5 NKJV

Every day we're faced with multiple opportunities to choose to do what's right or what's wrong. But the decision is made much easier when we have already predetermined in our minds to do what's right. Spiritual growth begins in the mind, and it is in the mind that we decide what to do and when to do it. It is vitally important that our minds think on things that are true and noble and honorable (see Philippians 4:8). When we do, the issue of how to handle certain decisions is made simple. Our minds are already made up: to do that which is honorable to God.

I have used a little saying with my kids for many years that simply goes like this: "Do what's right." As they've grown, "Do what's right" has taken on a much deeper meaning. Where it used to mean "don't take a cookie from the cookie jar," now it means "don't fall into the trappings of sin and selfishness that can take you further away than you ever planned."

Our bodies can't do anything our brains don't tell them to do, so living a lifestyle of worship begins with the mind.

I desire to live righteously before You, Father. Consecrate my mind.

All Creation Sings

Sing a new song to the LORD! Let the whole earth sing to the LORD! Let the heavens be glad, and the earth rejoice! Let the sea and everything in it shout his praise! Let the fields and their crops burst out with joy! Let the trees of the forest sing for joy before the LORD.

PSALM 96:1, 11–13

I am certainly not what you would call a "flower child" or a "tree hugger," but I do enjoy the beauty of nature. Have you ever taken the time to sit out in the woods or on an empty beach somewhere and just listen? Not to the sound of your own voice or what's playing in your headphones, but to the song of creation?

Creation makes music of its own, and I would venture to say it's the most beautiful music of all. And the song nature sings brings glory to the Firstborn of all creation, the Creator Himself, the Lord Jesus.

I love these words of Nehemiah: "You alone are the Lord. You made the heavens, even the highest heavens, and all their starry host, the earth and all that is on it, the seas and all that is in them. You give life to everything, and the multitudes of heaven worship you" (Nehemiah 9:6 NIV).

Let's join the song of creation today and sing our praises to the Lord!

I join my voice with creation today, creator God, in singing Your praises!

Worship through the Suffering

In his kindness God called you to share in his eternal glory by means of Christ Jesus. So after you have suffered a little while, he will restore, support, and strengthen you, and he will place you on a firm foundation.

1 PETER 5:10

Have you ever read the book of Job? It's a fascinating story about a man whom God allowed Satan to attack unmercifully in order to show he had a true heart of worship and devotion to God. We know this from the account of the story. The only problem is, Job didn't know this. So a huge part of the book is about Job's questioning why so many terrible things were happening to him.

Have you ever wondered why bad things happen to good people? One of the reasons God allows suffering in our lives is so that we might have a deeper and more accurate knowledge of God. Through suffering we learn that God's character never changes. God is good and just. We also learn that God is trustworthy. He knows our every need and is our great provider. And lastly, God is sovereign. He is in control and knows our situation. Our job is like that of Job: simply worship Him and trust Him.

Thank You for reminding me, Lord, that You are in control. You are utterly trustworthy and have my best interests at heart.

Under Rowing for His Glory

Anyone who wants to serve me must follow me, because my servants must be where I am. And the Father will honor anyone who serves me.

JOHN 12:26

The apostle Paul viewed himself as a slave of Jesus Christ. Listen to his words from his first letter to the Corinthians: "Let a man so consider us, as servants of Christ and stewards of the mysteries of God" (1 Corinthians 4:1 NKJV). I love the Greek word he uses for *servants*: It literally means "under rower." It gives us the picture of the old Roman slaves who were chained to the oars underneath the Roman galley ships and whose job was simply to row. Sometimes they would row fast, other times they would row slowly, and most of the time they didn't even know their own destination. Their job was simply to row.

In his life in Christ, Paul viewed himself as an under rower. As a worshiper and servant of the Most High God, he wanted to simply live as one who would be found faithful and trustworthy—rowing wherever the Spirit led him.

As worshipers we should adopt the same mind-set. Are we willing to go where He sends us? To do whatever He asks?

Father, You are my Lord and Master. May the set of my soul be like Paul's. I am a servant of Christ. Send me where You want me to go.

Gifted to Worship

Each of you should use whatever gift you have received to serve others, as faithful stewards of God's grace in its various forms. If anyone speaks, they should do so as one who speaks the very words of God. If anyone serves, they should do so with the strength God provides, so that in all things God may be praised through Jesus Christ.

I PETER 4:10–11 NIV

We are all gifted in unique ways. And there is a great diversity of gifts that God equips within us. But, as Paul reminds us in 1 Corinthians, even though we celebrate our different spiritual gifts, we all serve and worship the same Lord. Each of us is gifted so that the Holy Spirit can manifest Himself through our lives for the profit of all.

Some of you have the gift of wisdom. Others have the gift of giant faith, still others discernment, healing, prophecy, and tongues. But it is the Spirit of God who works in and through all of us to exhort and encourage one another, and to lead others to Him.

It is a beautiful thing to watch believers operate effortlessly in their gifting. It's not something they have to try to do. It just happens naturally. And as my pastor used to say, "In everything natural, be spiritual. In everything spiritual, be natural."

Thank You for the spiritual gifts You've bestowed on Your people, Lord! Every one of them is vital to the body of Christ.

Ignorance Is Bliss

I have hidden your word in my heart, that I might not sin against you. . . . Your word is a lamp to guide my feet and a light for my path.

PSALM 119:11, 105

Ignorance is bliss, or so they say. I recently heard some stats on how few Americans actually know the name of our vice president. It's shocking how many people are uninformed about basic things, especially when a world of knowledge is at our fingertips with the Internet.

So why is it that we choose to remain ignorant of so many things, especially those that are spiritual in nature? The pathway to deeper understanding is not by way of Google, but by way of obedience to the Word of God. Listen to the words of Jesus: "If anyone wills to do His will, he shall know concerning the doctrine, whether it is from God" (John 7:17 NKJV). In other words, if you and I are serious about growing closer to God and wanting to do His will, God will disclose the meaning of His Word to us. It's not a matter of if but when.

Immerse yourself in the reading and study of His Word. Ask God to reveal to you the hidden meanings, and let the words of life transform you. Seek Him today and worship Him in all you do.

God, I'm serious about doing Your will and drawing closer to You. May I be faithful to read and meditate on Your Word daily.

When Evil
Is at Your Door

The LORD is my light and my salvation—so why should I be afraid?
The LORD is my fortress, protecting me from danger, so why should
I tremble?

PSALM 27:1

Evil is all around us. We see it on the news every day. Just recently it hit us close to home when a local TV station employee shot and killed a reporter and her cameraman in cold blood as she was conducting a live interview. We watched in horror as we witnessed evil personified. Who knows if the gunman was possessed or just overcome with rage, but there is no denying we live in a world that is filled with evil.

Satan is not happy to be on the losing side, so he is roaming the earth seeking whom he may cause to sin, to stumble, and to fail. Often his fingerprints include violence and sexual perversion. However, we worship Jesus, the King of kings and Lord of lords. He holds all power over evil. In Him is the light and the life of salvation. We don't need to cower in fear. We have this promise in His Word: "If you make the Lord your refuge, if you make the Most High your shelter, no evil will conquer you; no plague will come near your home. For he will order his angels to protect you wherever you go" (Psalm 91:9–11).

I don't need to cower in fear or be overcome by worry, God Most High, for I am safe in the shelter of Your arms.

Have You Ever Had a Personal Encounter with God?

Inside the Tent of Meeting, the LORD would speak to Moses face to face, as one speaks to a friend.

EXODUS 33:11

Moses met with God face-to-face. Just think about that. The thought is unbelievable. The Bible tells us that Moses had regular conversations with God. But when we look closer, we see that many of these conversations took place on a mountaintop and after he had spent much time alone in God's presence. Keep in mind that Moses was the leader of a people over a million strong in number. I'm sure he had just a few things going on! But nothing took precedence over his time with God.

Martin Luther was quoted as having said, "I have so much to do today that I cannot afford to spend less than three hours in prayer." Most of us don't even spend three minutes a day in prayer. And yet that is where we find real peace from God in the middle of the chaos and hear His voice above the noise.

Do you want to worship God more intimately? Do you want to have an encounter with God that is unforgettable? Then be like Moses. Get away from the noise of life, even if it's just a little while each day. Seek His face and then open your ears. God still speaks.

Help me to get away from the noise each day, Lord, and take time to seek Your face.

Who Am I, That You Would Love Me?

O LORD, what are human beings that you should notice them, mere mortals that you should think about them?

PSALM 144:3

When I consider all that God has made and all that He has done, it has a tendency to make me feel insignificant. When I consider the heavens and the vast expanses of the universe, I feel pretty small. When I consider all of the wonders of this earth and the powers of nature, I feel weak and helpless.

David considered these same things in Psalm 8: "When I consider Your heavens, the work of Your fingers . . . what is man that You are mindful of him, and the son of man that You visit him? For You have made him a little lower than the angels, and You have crowned him with glory and honor" (Psalm 8:3–5 NKJV). Wow! God has given mankind dominion over all the wonder and power and glory of all the universe and creation, and placed us just below His own angels!

We have two takeaways today: (1) to take care of His creation, and (2) to worship Him as Creator. We have a responsibility to be good stewards of all God has made, and we have the privilege to worship the One who made it all!

Blessed Creator, thank You for this beautiful earth. Help me to be a good steward of its resources.

Sing to God!

Let the godly sing for joy to the LORD; it is fitting for the pure to praise him. Praise the LORD with melodies on the lyre; make music for him on the ten-stringed harp. Sing a new song of praise to him; play skillfully on the harp, and sing with joy.

PSALM 33:1–3

I encourage you today to start each day with praise to the Lord. It's just a great way to help you remember, first and foremost, who is worthy of your heart's affection and your mind's attention.

There's a variety of ways in which we can praise the Lord, but do you ever sing a song to Him? I know you do when you worship corporately together on Sunday mornings, but I mean, by yourself? There have been times when I've sung my heart out to the Lord in my car and have gotten some strange looks from the drivers in the other lane, but it was worth it!

Psalm 105 says, "Oh, give thanks to the Lord! Call upon His name; make known His deeds among the peoples! Sing to Him, sing psalms to Him; talk of all His wondrous works!" (1–2 NKJV). Maybe you should try that today! It's not the quality of your voice that matters; it's the praise from your heart that He wants to hear.

Lord, I'm going to sing Your praises out loud today with a thankful heart!

Character Matters

We can rejoice, too, when we run into problems and trials, for we know that they help us develop endurance. And endurance develops strength of character, and character strengthens our confident hope of salvation.

ROMANS 5:3–4

Who in your life would you say are people of character? Nine times out of ten, people with character got that way because they've been through the fire a few times. They have trudged through, climbed over, and crawled under the trials of life, and through it all they have developed character.

Character doesn't come overnight. There's a price to be paid. To be a person of character doesn't just mean that you have high moral standards or are honest in your dealings with others and striving to remain above reproach. Being a person of character also means that you can meet the demands of reality. Of course, defining our own reality can be quite difficult at times, but it starts with honesty—honesty about our strengths and our weaknesses. Character reveals who you really are in every situation, but it is especially noticeable when times get tough. Worshipers have strong character.

Jesus is God, so when He walked this earth in human form, He was in the flesh but still had no character flaws. He lived a sinless life. So if you want the perfect model for strong character, look to Jesus first. And then worship Him as God.

Help me to respond with grace to Your work in my life, Lord Jesus. Develop in me the character of Christ.

Worship the Omnipotent, Omnipresent, Omniscient God

I can never escape from your Spirit! I can never get away from your presence! . . . If I ride the wings of the morning, if I dwell by the farthest oceans, even there your hand will guide me, and your strength will support me.

PSALM 139:7, 9–10

Omnipotent—all-powerful. This word can only be used to describe God Almighty, the Creator of all. Think about it: Nothing and no one else can be called omnipotent. Everything and everyone has their limits, except God. It is healthy to fear such a powerful God, but only if you fear Him in such a way that it drives you to worship Him at His feet in holy reverence.

God is also omnipresent—present everywhere. He is able to hear the prayers of His children in China and be present at a worship service in Virginia at the same time. Wherever we may be, we are always in His watchful care and His presence is always near.

Not only is God omnipotent and omnipresent, He is omniscient—all-seeing and all-knowing. Wow! Do you ever consider this during your day, that God knows every thought you think, hears every word you speak, and sees everything you do? And yet, despite our many mess-ups, He still loves us more than we could possibly imagine!

Focus your heart's affection and your mind's attention on God alone. Let Him receive the full adoration of your heart.

You are amazing, God! I give You my praise and adoration today.

Worship in the Waiting

I am confident I will see the LORD's goodness while I am here in the land of the living. Wait patiently for the LORD. Be brave and courageous. Yes, wait patiently for the LORD.

PSALM 27:13–14

Do you ever feel like your prayers are just hitting the ceiling? That God doesn't hear you? Maybe you feel like God has more important things to deal with than you and your problems. Or perhaps you feel abandoned by the Lord.

I want to encourage you not to lose heart today. Continue to worship the Lord while you wait on Him. He holds the answers to your issues, and He is the source of your strength even when you've grown weary. He loves you and cares for you and has your best interests at heart. So be patient. Learn to rest in the restlessness of the waiting period. And then, be willing to let go of the life you have planned for yourself, in order to accept the life God has planned for you.

"Those who wait on the Lord shall renew their strength; they shall mount up with wings like eagles, they shall run and not be weary, they shall walk and not faint" (Isaiah 40:31 NKJV). Wait on the Lord—and continue to worship.

You always hear my prayers, Lord, even when I don't get the answers I want in the time frame I want them. I trust You in this waiting period. Renew my strength as I wait upon You.

Loving Your Enemies

Never pay back evil with more evil. Do things in such a way that everyone can see you are honorable. Do all that you can to live in peace with everyone.

ROMANS 12:17–18

It's much easier to love people whom we like. It's even manageable to love people whom we don't like. But to love those who are our outright enemies?

In Matthew 5:44 Jesus tells us to love our enemies and bless those who curse us. He even tells us to "do good to those who hate you, and pray for those who spitefully use you and persecute you" (Matthew 5:44 NKJV). And in the book of Proverbs we are told, "If your enemies are hungry, give them food to eat. If they are thirsty, give them water to drink. You will heap burning coals of shame on their heads, and the Lord will reward you" (25:21–22).

In order to do this, we have to have God in our lives. Only the grace of the Lord Jesus can cause us to actually love our enemies. This is a totally unnatural response to a difficult situation. But you know what happens when we do? We become more intimate worshipers of Jesus.

So part of living a lifestyle of worship is learning to love those who don't love us, even going out of our way to bless those who curse us. Easier said than done, but the end results can be incredibly rewarding.

Help me, Lord, to love my enemies and look for opportunities to bless them.

Worship for a Lifetime

The generous will prosper; those who refresh others will themselves be refreshed.

PROVERBS 11:25

Picture yourself as a seventy-five-year-old. Life is slower. The crazy pace of e-mails, texts, phone calls, and meetings is now tucked away in your memory, and you have much more time to sit and to reflect. What kind of memories do you think you will have at that age? What kinds of relationships will still be intact in your life? What sorts of regrets do you think you'll have?

One way to be certain you live a life that is full of adventure and devoid of regrets is to live each and every moment to the glory of God. It's amazing what happens when your focus is first to love God with all your heart. This keeps your life clean from habitual sin. It keeps your relationships with others properly focused. And it keeps your heart and mind on the right priorities day in and day out.

If you make worship a lifestyle for a lifetime, your life will be blessed, and when you get to the end, you will be able to look back and realize that your life has blessed many others. But most importantly, you will realize that your life has been well-spent pleasing God.

Lord, help me to make loving You the focus of my heart each and every day.

Integrity on Display

People with integrity walk safely, but those who follow crooked paths will be exposed.

PROVERBS 10:9

It is a well-known fact that when Billy Graham would arrive in a town to hold a crusade, the first thing he would do in his hotel room was unplug the TV. Cliff Barrows would place a towel over the TV and then put a picture of his family on top of the towel. Both of these great men of God would do this for the sole purpose of maintaining integrity and purity during the crusade. Having traveled a great deal, I so appreciate this about these men. It shows their commitment to what the Bible commands ministers to be: above reproach.

Integrity is something that must be practiced in front of people and behind closed doors alike. As worshipers, we must make absolute integrity the compass that guides our decisions in everything we do, and we must surround ourselves with people who are committed to do the same.

What is the compass for integrity? The Word of God. That is your true authority and guide for every decision you make in life. It is what will point you toward wisdom and give you the knowledge to live a life of integrity. So strive for integrity in all areas of your life: your business, your hobbies, your relationships, your finances, and most of all your walk with Jesus.

Lord, help me to live in a way that honors You in public and in private.

To Do or To Be . . .
That Is the Question

Those who obey God's word truly show how completely they love him. That is how we know we are living in him. Those who say they live in God should live their lives as Jesus did.

1 JOHN 2:5–6

You have probably heard it said before, but it remains true: It's just as important, or even more important, to concentrate on *who* we are than on *what* we are. All of us want to be successful in our own related fields. We want to go to our grave one day having accomplished something. But what does that really mean? Does it mean we have grown rich? Does it mean we own a huge business? Or could it mean simply that we have become the man or woman God intended us to be?

Oswald Chambers said: "The only thing that exceeds right-doing is right-being." The only way to *be* right in God's eyes is to live a life of worship of Him and obedience to His Word. So, in your efforts to succeed in this world, remember that the greatest success comes when we concentrate on simply *being* the person God wants us to be in all areas of life.

Lord, make me into the person You want me to be!

I Am Not Ashamed

I have not been afraid to speak out, as you, O LORD, well know. I have not kept the good news of your justice hidden in my heart; I have talked about your faithfulness and saving power.

PSALM 40:9–10

I don't know about you, but I find great inspiration from those who boldly live out their faith and are willing to die for their Savior. They are the ones who can quote Romans 1:16 without any reservation: "For I am not ashamed of the gospel of Christ, for it is the power of God to salvation for everyone who believes, for the Jew first and also for the Greek" (NKJV).

Paul reminds us in this verse that the good news of Jesus is for Jews and Gentiles alike. In other words, the salvation of Christ is for everyone. But the point is that Paul was not afraid to let anyone and everyone know about it. In fact, he couldn't help but tell everyone about it, even the Romans, who could kill him for sharing the gospel. This good news is the salvation of every worshiper. And it should be the passion of every worshiper to boldly proclaim it.

I am not ashamed of the gospel, Lord Jesus! If I'm ever given the opportunity, I pray that You'll give me the courage to boldly declare my faith.

Peace That Passes All Understanding

You will keep in perfect peace all who trust in you, all whose thoughts are fixed on you! Trust in the LORD always, for the LORD GOD is the eternal Rock.

ISAIAH 26:3–4

The most frustrated people in the world are those who can't make up their minds. Philippians 4:6–7 tells us: "Be anxious for nothing, but in everything by prayer and supplication, with thanksgiving, let your requests be made known to God; and the peace of God, which surpasses all understanding, will guard your hearts and minds through Christ Jesus" (NKJV).

What's the opposite of peace? Worry. It's interesting to note that the Greek word for anxious means to have a "mind divided" between good thoughts and bad thoughts. It is those destructive thoughts that choke out the power of God's Word working in and through our daily lives.

So Paul encourages us not to allow our minds to get divided over anything. Rather, with a focused mind, seek God's help in everything. And in so doing, the peace of God will reign in our lives so strongly that we won't even be able to describe it in human terms. And it is this peace that will guard our hearts from straying and keep our minds sharp and decisive.

God, help me to keep my thoughts focused on You, and not to allow my mind to be divided. Thank You for the peace that You give as I do so.

The Bread of Life

Jesus replied, "I am the bread of life. Whoever comes to me will never be hungry again. Whoever believes in me will never be thirsty."

JOHN 6:35

I think one of my favorite things in the world to eat is piping-hot New England clam chowder in a sourdough bread bowl. I just love that bread. I know they say it's not good for you, but what is probably bad for my health sure does nourish my heart: It makes me very happy!

Jesus referred to Himself as the Bread of Life. When He first made that proclamation, all the religious crowd sneered at Him because they thought He was literally talking about the eating of His own flesh. But they also knew He was referencing the Torah—the books of Moses—which they often referred to as "bread" because within it was contained the words of life.

So, in essence, what Jesus was saying when He called Himself the "bread of life" is that He is the fulfillment of the promise of a messiah in the Torah, and that He is the giver of life to all who worship Him and believe in Him. "I am the living bread that came down from heaven. Anyone who eats this bread will live forever; and this bread, which I will offer so the world may live, is my flesh" (John 6:51).

Thank You, precious Savior, for being the Bread of Life. In You I have life and every need of mine is met.

Worshipers, Repent!

The LORD says, "Turn to me now, while there is time. Give me your hearts. Come with fasting, weeping, and mourning. Don't tear your clothing in your grief, but tear your hearts instead." Return to the LORD your God, for he is merciful and compassionate, slow to get angry and filled with unfailing love. He is eager to relent and not punish.

JOEL 2:12–13

We live in a culture that is totally self-absorbed. Even criminals are told they can blame their irresponsible, immoral behavior on traumatic events in their past or chalk it up to being victimized in some way. In this day and age, it seems that no one is truly at fault, because there is always another reason or person to blame. But God calls out sinners to repent. To turn from their wicked ways. To take responsibility for their own sins.

Perhaps one of the things that could turn our culture away from its self-absorption would be for us all to take responsibility for our wrongdoings. Have the courage to say we are sorry. Stand up and admit when we are wrong. We must get honest with ourselves about sin. We are not fooling God. He already knows our hearts. So if we are going to live a lifestyle of worship, then we must humble ourselves before God and repent.

O Lord, may I always be quick to repent and quick to take responsibility for my own actions.

Worship with Purpose

I was glad when they said to me, "Let us go to the house of the Lord."

PSALM 122:1

Do you ever sit in church and wonder what the purpose of church is? Did you know that the reason we gather together each week to sing praises and study God's Word goes back to the beginning of faith itself? Abraham worshiped God with his family. Moses would gather the people of God together to worship and hear the law of God. Joshua did the same, as well as many others throughout Scripture, and as Christians we have been doing it ever since.

So, what's the purpose of gathering for worship? To draw near to the presence of God as His children. Yes, we learn from His Word, and yes, we sing songs of praise and give offerings and celebrate baptisms. But primarily, we gather to experience His presence among us. For it is in the presence of God Almighty that hardened hearts are broken, broken lives are mended, and mended souls are encouraged. The prophet Hosea drives this truth home: "Come, let us return to the Lord. . . . In just a short time he will restore us, so that we may live in his presence" (Hosea 6:1–2).

Worship the Lord with the purpose of dwelling in His presence. It will change you forever.

Heavenly Father, may I never grow weary of gathering in Your house with other believers!

Worship God
by Listening to Others

A truly wise person uses few words; a person with understanding is even-tempered.

PROVERBS 17:27

Worship is loving God. And we worship Him by loving and serving others, as well. One of the best ways to serve others is to simply listen to them. Everyone wants three things: to be heard, to be respected, and to be understood. It's amazing how much more others respect us when we simply spend a few moments listening to them. To truly listen to others is to show our love for them.

Jesus did this better than anyone. He would listen to people, then point them to the truth. They would hear, and be changed forever.

You've probably heard it said before that we have two ears and one mouth, so we should listen twice as much as we speak. The Bible says something similar when James reminds us, "Be quick to listen, slow to speak and slow to get angry" (James 1:19). One way we can improve our lifestyle of worship is to talk less and listen more. Do you want to worship God more deeply and earn the right to be heard at the same time? Then practice the art of opening your ears to others and truly listening to them.

This isn't always easy, Lord, but please help me to talk less and listen more.

Worship Him Completely

May the God of peace make you holy in every way, and may your whole spirit and soul and body be kept blameless until our Lord Jesus Christ comes again. God will make this happen, for he who calls you is faithful.

1 THESSALONIANS 5:23–24

I recently received a letter from a friend who was dying. The last words that she shared with me were from Philippians 1:6: "Being confident of this very thing, that He who has begun a good work in you will complete it until the day of Jesus Christ" (NKJV).

One of the most comforting things about our salvation is the fact that it is complete and it is eternal. When God starts something, He finishes it. So when His Spirit came to dwell in your heart, it wasn't for just a moment in time or for a season; it was for eternity. The salvation that came to you on the day you met Jesus will hold you and keep you forever!

This should not only give us comfort, but it should also give us confidence. We can live boldly for God and loudly sing our praises of Him, because He is the one who holds our todays and our tomorrows in His hands. In the words of a friend of mine: "Our redemption has been sealed." Hallelujah!

I praise You and thank You for Your salvation, Lord Jesus! I'm grateful that You will never let me go.

Worship God as a Self-Feeder

Let the message about Christ, in all its richness, fill your lives.

COLOSSIANS 3:16

One of the small joys of parenting comes when your children have matured enough to feed themselves. No longer are you having to hover over their high chair with a baby spoon filled with blended vegetable "ick," because they can now choose, chew, and swallow their own bites of food. However, if they ate only one meal a week, they would probably starve, or at the very least be extremely malnourished and unhealthy.

Sadly, many Christians treat their own spiritual growth this way. They assume it's enough to go to church once a week, but they don't realize they're starving themselves. Remember this: The key to your spiritual maturity and lifestyle of worship is to become a self-feeder. One sermon on a Sunday morning is never enough. You must dive into the Word of God yourself. Seek His face each day of every week! Learn to worship the Lord beyond just a few songs on Sunday. You will find that the more you do this, the more hungry you become for more of Him. And we have His promise that "he satisfies the thirsty and fills the hungry with good things" (Psalm 107:9).

Save me, Lord, from neglecting to feed myself spiritually. May I be faithful every day to get into the Word and seek You diligently, in addition to meeting with other believers on Sunday morning.

Worship God the Creator

This is what the LORD says—your Redeemer and Creator: "I am the LORD, who made all things. I alone stretched out the heavens. Who was with me when I made the earth?"

ISAIAH 44:24

Have you ever stopped to think just how creative God is? Recently I returned from Phoenix. Before that I was in San Francisco. Previous to that I was in Florida, and I live in Virginia. Four distinct areas of our country, all beautiful, but all completely different. Then, of course, there's the matchless beauty of the mountains and the oceans and everything in between. Not to mention all the species of animals and birds of the air. Oh! and then there are the fish in the ocean and the uncharted world of outer space. God's creativity is endless. And last but not least, there are the seven billion people on this planet, and not one of us has the same DNA or even fingerprint! God's creativity is unbelievable!

So let me ask you something: If the God we worship is that creative, don't you reckon He's got a pretty good plan for your life, as well? If the God who could create so much beauty and variety is the Lord of your life, just think what He can do in and through you!

Thank You for that reminder, Father. I love how creative You are, and I trust Your amazing plan for my life.

Scattered, Smothered, Covered

He will cover you with his feathers. He will shelter you with his wings. His faithful promises are your armor and protection.

PSALM 91:4

I love the Waffle House. Their food makes me happy. Not only can you get waffles there, but you can order hash browns any way you want them. Sometimes I hear people get them scattered, smothered, and covered. That means broken apart, smothered in cheese, and covered with onions.

In an odd sort of way, this is a great picture of the Church. We are one body, with one Savior. Yet we are scattered all over the world, numbering in the hundreds of millions. "There are many parts, but only one body" (1 Corinthians 12:20).

We are smothered, in a good way, by His Holy Spirit. It is the Spirit of God that protects us and guides us all throughout each day. "He has given us the Holy Spirit to fill our hearts with his love" (Romans 5:5). May we listen to His guidance and hear His voice in all things.

And finally, we are covered by the blood of Jesus. It is His love and His sacrifice that holds us and keeps us for all eternity. "You have obeyed him and have been cleansed by the blood of Jesus Christ" (1 Peter 1:2).

I know it may sound silly, but sometimes even the way we order our hash browns can prompt us to worship the King!

I praise You, my King, for Your beautiful plan for the Church, the body of Christ!

Honoring God with Our Worship

O LORD, I will honor and praise your name, for you are my God. You do such wonderful things! You planned them long ago, and now you have accomplished them.

ISAIAH 25:1

I saw a bumper sticker the other day that simply said "Honor yourself." Although it's biblical to have a positive self-image and to treat your body as a temple of the Lord, I do believe that we have gone way overboard in our culture with this mind-set. The thought is always to look out for "number one" before we consider anyone else. If you question this, then go stand in line at a Toys "R" Us during the Christmas rush. Or just drive down a highway during rush hour in any major city.

We live in a selfish society, and it's contagious. We can so easily get caught up in honoring ourselves that we ignore others, and worse yet, turn our backs on God. I know I've been guilty of this many times.

So here is our worship challenge for the day: Honor the Lord before honoring ourselves. It will not come naturally, but we need to see ourselves for who we are: servants of the Most High God. Ironically, when we focus our attention and affection on Him, He ends up honoring us back! Isn't that just like God?

Help me to remember today, Lord God, that I am Your servant and I should honor You in all my ways.

Living the Life of Worship

The LORD is my strength and shield. I trust him with all my heart. He helps me, and my heart is filled with joy. I burst out in songs of thanksgiving.

PSALM 28:7

The most joyful people on earth are those who have discovered the beauty of living completely for Jesus. Their focus is no longer pulled aside by distractions, and they are free of all pretense. Just pure hearts seeking the Lord each and every day and trying to please Him alone. I have discovered these people have learned four key things: First, they have learned to really live. They don't just exist—they live an abundant, thriving, adventurous life for Christ.

Second, they have learned to lead. Because they follow Christ alone, their boldness is contagious and their zeal is inspiring. Third, they have learned to laugh. Their joy is complete and guilt-free. They can laugh, not at others' expense, but in pure fun. And, they can laugh at themselves. Finally, they have learned to love. They have discovered the unconditional love of Jesus and are able to see every person through the lens of God's true love.

Don't you want to be one of these people? Then do it! Surrender your life to worshiping Jesus as a lifestyle.

Father, I want this joyful, abundant life of worship. As I surrender to You, I pray that You will work this out in me.

Worship with the Right Motive

When you give to someone in need, don't let your left hand know what your right hand is doing. Give your gifts in private, and your Father, who sees everything, will reward you.

MATTHEW 6:3–4

It's important always to do the right thing. But we worship a God who doesn't just want us to do the right things; He wants us to do the right things in the right way. We must be careful to check our motives before our actions. In God's eyes, *how* something is done is as important as *what* is done. What is our motive for doing what we do? Is it money that is motivating us? Is it power? Success? The approval and applause of others? For the worshiper of God, our motive behind everything we do should be to glorify the Lord. "Whatever you do, do it heartily, as to the Lord and not to men" (Colossians 3:23 NKJV).

So as you set your goals, as you go to church, as you participate in projects, even as you exercise, make sure your motive is to bring glory to God in all your endeavors. Remember, you are here on this earth to worship God. What is your motive today? Let a pure love for God motivate all you do.

Examine my motives, Father. May nothing but love for You drive me today.

Do a Little Dance for Jesus

You have turned my mourning into joyful dancing. You have taken away my clothes of mourning and clothed me with joy, that I might sing praises to you and not be silent. O LORD my God, I will give you thanks forever!

PSALM 30:11–12

When David brought the ark of the covenant from the house of Obed-Edom to the city of Jerusalem, he followed explicitly the instructions the Lord gave Moses on the proper way to transport the ark. The Levites carried it using designated poles, and sacrifices were made literally every six paces. That was a slow trip, but a worshipful one. When the ark finally entered Jerusalem, the Bible says that David danced before the Lord with all his might. He was overcome with joy at the return of the Lord's presence to the Holy City. It was a tremendous celebration marked by joy and triumph rather than royal pomp and pageantry. As the anointed king, David had no doubt in his mind and heart that God had placed him there, so he worshiped the Lord with reckless abandon and with a grateful spirit.

What's holding us back from following David's example? God is on His throne and He has blessed us abundantly, so let's dance before Him and worship Him with grateful hearts!

Dear Lord, You've blessed me so richly. I'm going to do a little dance for You!

Worshiping God with Healthy Eyes

Your eye is like a lamp that provides light for your body. When your eye is healthy, your whole body is filled with light.

MATTHEW 6:22

It is a fact that where my eyes are is where my attention lies. For instance, if my child is talking to me and my eyes are on my phone, then the phone is still winning my attention over my child. If I'm driving and my attention is caught by something other than the road, the car will veer toward what my eyes are gazing at.

No doubt Jesus was alluding to this when He told us in Luke 11:34, "Your eye is the lamp of your body. When your eyes are healthy, your whole body also is full of light. But when they are unhealthy, your body also is full of darkness" (NIV). In other words, if we keep our eyes on that which is holy, our lives will be a light in a dark world, but if we get distracted and fix our eyes on that which is sinful, then we darken not only our own souls but those around us as well. So as we strive toward a lifestyle of worship, let's make wise daily choices to protect our eyes from all things impure and ungodly and keep them healthy by focusing on that which is pure and holy.

Help me, heavenly Father, to keep my eyes healthy and full of light, that I might live a pure life of worship before You.

It's All about the Cross

As for me, may I never boast about anything except the cross of our Lord Jesus Christ. Because of that cross, my interest in this world has been crucified, and the world's interest in me has also died.

GALATIANS 6:14

How much joy does the cross give you? Do you ever find yourself just boasting about the victory Christ has given you because of His victory over the cross? Or do you boast instead of your latest business deal or your low golf score?

Paul was so consumed with the cross of Jesus that he could boast about that and that alone. Everything else was secondary in his life; the salvation and the hope that Jesus provided him at the cross was his greatest joy in life. This reminds me of a song I recorded a few years ago: "Our only boast is the cross, all our hope is Christ in us. He was crucified and raised and forever we will praise the living God." It was on the cross that Jesus—God in the flesh, the personification of love itself—gave Himself up for you and for me, because He loves us.

We tend to boast, or glory in, that which gives us the most delight and in that which brings us success. Well, the cross should delight us because it is our hope—so boast in that today!

I delight in Your cross today, Lord Jesus, and I make it my boast!

Water for Worshipers

Blessed are those who trust in the LORD and have made the LORD their hope and confidence. They are like trees planted along a riverbank, with roots that reach deep into the water. Such trees are not bothered by the heat or worried by long months of drought. Their leaves stay green, and they never stop producing fruit.

JEREMIAH 17:7–8

When I was a kid, my family lived in the northern plains area of the country. We traveled quite a bit and used to play a game we created called Lake. It's a simple game. Whenever you see a lake, you yell, "Lake!"—and if you yell first, you get the point. Well, it didn't take me long as a child to learn that whenever I saw a clump of trees in those plains, water was nearby. That's because water is the life-giver to trees.

It's the same picture we see in Psalm 1:3, where the writer describes for us the identity of one who lives a lifestyle of worship. Those who delight themselves in the Lord and meditate on His Word are "like a tree planted by the rivers of water" (Psalm 1:3 NKJV). The tree gets its nourishment from the water, just as the worshiper gets his nourishment from the Word of God. It is the constant supply of God's grace and wisdom that keeps a person's soul healthy and strong. Let's stay in His Word and let our souls prosper!

Help me to be vigilant, Father, to nourish my soul in the Word.

The Successful Worshiper

The godly will flourish like palm trees and grow strong like the cedars of Lebanon. For they are transplanted to the LORD's own house. They flourish in the courts of our God. Even in old age they will still produce fruit; they will remain vital and green.

PSALM 92:12–14

The blessed life is the life that delights in the Word of God and the things of God. As we learned from Psalm 1:3 in the previous entry, that life is like a tree planted near rivers of water. It is a life of worship. It is a healthy and prosperous life. You know why? Because a tree planted near the water is able to put roots deep into the soil and constantly draw nutrients from it. That's why it is crucial that you and I stay in the Word of God.

This same verse tells us that our days will be fruitful and our lives will bring prosperity. But let's keep in mind that prosperity in the eyes of God is not the same as the prosperity that exists in the eyes of man. Being fruitful doesn't necessarily mean being wealthy. Success doesn't always equate to riches. The list is long of great people who lived extraordinary lives but who did so without much money or because they gave all they had away. So if you want to live a blessed life, start at verse three in Psalm 1. Plant yourself in the Word of God, then see where He leads you.

Yes, Lord, I will plant myself in Your Word.

Total Renovation

Don't copy the behavior and customs of this world, but let God transform you into a new person by changing the way you think. Then you will learn to know God's will for you, which is good and pleasing and perfect.

ROMANS 12:2

Have you ever renovated a part of your home or office? If you have, then you know it takes several major steps to accomplish it. It starts with the vision for what you want to change, then it leads to the plans and drawings so you can see that vision on paper. That, in turn, leads to the tearing down of the old in order to make way for the new, and finally, the construction and finished product.

In the same way, God changes us from the inside out when we renovate or transform our thought lives from one that has been "conformed to this world" to one that is godly. Sincere worship begins in the mind. And just like in renovating a home, we must allow God to tear down the old walls of worldly thinking in order to clean us up and renew our thoughts on that which is pure and honoring to Him. We must cast "down arguments and every high thing that exalts itself against the knowledge of God, bringing every thought into captivity to the obedience of Christ" (2 Corinthians 10:5 NKJV).

I give You free rein, Master Builder, to renovate and transform my soul for Your glory.

Worshiping God from Our Knees

Come, let us worship and bow down. Let us kneel before the Lord our maker, for he is our God.

PSALM 95:6–7

We've seen it many times in movies or pictures: When one is brought into the presence of royalty or greatness, the first thing they do is bow to their knees in reverence and humility. In Ephesians 3:14, Paul mentions praying from a posture of bowing his knees: "When I think of all this, I fall to my knees and pray to the Father." This position of utmost humility was in contrast to the more normal posture of prayer in that culture in which they would pray standing with hands raised up. And yet, all through Scripture we see this posture—kneeling to pray. From Solomon's dedication of the temple to Jesus in the garden, praying from the knees is shown as a definite sign of humility before the Lord.

I want to encourage you, if you are physically able, to make kneeling before the Lord a common practice in your life. There is just something about that act that immediately places us in a position of service before our Lord. And when we humble ourselves before Him on our knees, He makes us that much stronger when we stand.

I gladly get down on my knees right now and offer You my worship and praise, gracious heavenly Father!

No More Night, No More Pain

He will wipe every tear from their eyes, and there will be no more death or sorrow or crying or pain. All these things are gone forever.

REVELATION 21:4

Do you ever dream about what heaven will be like? I think about it often. The Bible tells us much about heaven. Think about all the incredible sights we will behold: golden streets so pure that they are transparent, walls of jade, a crystal sea, jewels of every kind under our feet, angels everywhere, and loved ones to greet us. Can you just picture it?

But what about the intangibles? How about no more pain, no more tears, no more sorrow, no more loss? What about no more work, no more labor, no more stress, no more taxes! And then, of course, there will be no more night. The Son— S-O-N—will shine eternally, and we will live in the light and glory of His love for eternity. "The city has no need of sun or moon, for the glory of God illuminates the city, and the Lamb is its light" (Revelation 21:23).

But more than anything, we will worship Jesus unceasingly. Believer, don't you think it would be good practice for you to worship Him today? Don't wait for the wonders of heaven to discover the glories of worship!

I'm not going to wait till I get to heaven to worship my Savior. I praise and lift You high here on earth today!

How Can I Present My Body as a Living Sacrifice?

Do not let any part of your body become an instrument of evil to serve sin. Instead, give yourselves completely to God, for you were dead, but now you have new life. So use your whole body as an instrument to do what is right for the glory of God.

ROMANS 6:13

It almost sounds like a morbid thought, doesn't it? A living sacrifice? Yet that is the very phrase the apostle Paul uses in Romans 12:1. It is a reference to the Old Testament days when shepherds sacrificed sheep as an offering unto God. But when Jesus came, it all turned upside down. Now the Shepherd had offered Himself as a sacrifice for His sheep and the covenant of grace became reality.

So when Paul says we are to present our bodies as a living sacrifice, he literally means we are to present all that we are, all that we have, and all that we wish to be—our jobs, our future, our families, our goals, and our dreams—as an offering to God, so that He might use us the way He chooses, that He might break us where we need to be broken, and that He might mold us into the worshipers He created us to be.

Lord, I present my body to You today as a living sacrifice, along with all my hopes and dreams and aspirations. It's such a small price to pay compared to Your sacrifice on Calvary!

Watch Your Backhand

Be strong in the Lord and in his mighty power. Put on all of God's armor so that you will be able to stand firm against all strategies of the devil. For we are not fighting against flesh-and-blood enemies, but against evil rulers and authorities of the unseen world, against mighty powers in this dark world, and against evil spirits in the heavenly places.

EPHESIANS 6:10–12

It is a well-known fact that most tennis players have a weaker backhand than they do a forehand. When playing your opponent, you typically want to exploit that.

You know, Satan does the same thing to us in our own lives. He knows our weaknesses, and he does everything he can to exploit them. The Bible says he roams the earth "like a roaring lion, seeking whom he may devour" (1 Peter 5:8 NKJV). However, Paul reminds us in 2 Corinthians 12 that in our weakness we are made strong through the power of the Holy Spirit, who lives within us. So we need to understand and know our weaknesses.

Be aware that if you are weak in a certain area, Satan is going to come at you with every shot and from every angle. Then be aware that Jesus can handle anything Satan throws your way. So stay on the court, strive for godliness, and watch your backhand.

Father, help me to understand what my weaknesses are, and then help me to stand and be strong in the power of Your might. Protect me from my enemy.

Salvation: Past, Present, and Future

God saved us and called us to live a holy life. He did this, not because we deserved it, but because that was his plan from before the beginning of time—to show us his grace through Christ Jesus.

2 TIMOTHY 1:9

There are three words related to salvation that every worshiper should be able to define: *justification*, *sanctification*, and *glorification*. *Justification* means that you have been freed from the penalty of sin. This happens immediately, the moment Jesus saves you. *Sanctification* means that you are being freed from the power of sin. This happens progressively and daily as a believer when you stay close and pure before the Lord. And *glorification* means that you have been freed from the presence of sin. Obviously, because we live in a sin-filled world, glorification will happen in the future, when we are in the presence of God in glory.

It is the combination of these three words that brings us complete salvation in Christ from the moment we met Him, through the trouble of the day, and ultimately in heaven with Him forever. It is faith alone that gives us the ability to trust the Lord as our Savior, and it is the Lord Jesus alone who has the power to save us. Our faith in itself is a gift of God. Each day can become a new adventure when we live by faith.

Thank You, Jesus, for justifying me, sanctifying me, and one day glorifying me in heaven. I praise You for Your incredible plan of salvation!

Worship in the Failures

Create in me a clean heart, O God. Renew a loyal spirit within me.

PSALM 51:10

Have you ever felt like a failure? Have you ever messed up really bad, and everyone around you knew it? Remember the embarrassment? Remember the ridiculing looks, the scolding eyes?

King David felt that, too. He royally messed up his life when he sinned with Bathsheba. One wrong move led to another, and it soon brought down the wrath of God. David repented with all his heart, but he still had to face the consequences with his family, his friends, and even his own health. And he would endure the consequences for the rest of his life. Yet he turned back to the Lord and worshiped Him in his repentance. He blessed the Lord with his brokenness. And God forgave him, restored him, and rebuilt his life.

If you feel like a failure today, look to the life of David and remember to worship God through your failures. Begin with prayer—prayer that's from the heart, honest before God. Paul tells us in Colossians 4 to "continue earnestly" in prayer (4:2 NKJV). In other words, make it a commitment in your life. Practice it as a discipline.

Do we want God to use us in a major way? Do we want to accomplish something significant in our lives and see the world around us change? Then let's drop to our knees and start praying, frequently!

Help me, Father, to keep worshiping You even when I fail.

Is It Possible to Listen with Your Eyes?

Feed the hungry, and help those in trouble. Then your light will shine out from the darkness, and the darkness around you will be as bright as noon.

ISAIAH 58:10

There is much we can learn by hearing instruction. But that learning process is even more effective when those instructions come to life by way of pictures or video or demonstration. We are a visual people, and for many of us, we are able to grasp a concept more quickly when we see an example of it before us.

Jesus used word pictures and visuals all the time in His teaching. In one instance He said, "Lift up your eyes and look at the fields. . . . They are already white for harvest" (John 4:35 NKJV). It's a visual reminder to all of us that the world is ripe for the telling of the good news of the gospel.

As worshipers, our responsibility is to share the truth and love of the gospel. So I encourage you today to open your eyes and listen with them. Can you see the cry of the poor and the needy? Do you see the lonely weeping of the abused and abandoned? Do you see the pleading heart of that bitter person at work? Listen with your eyes, and the needs around you get louder.

O Lord, help me to listen with my eyes. Give me a heart of compassion for the hurting, and then lead me to act on it according to Your will.

Enjoy God Forever

Come, you who are blessed by my Father, inherit the Kingdom prepared for you from the creation of the world.

MATTHEW 25:34

It's a fact: There's a real place called heaven and there's a real place called hell. Every soul who has ever lived will end up in one of these two places. Psalm 1:4–5 gives us a clear picture of who will be where. "[The wicked] are like worthless chaff, scattered by the wind. They will be condemned at the time of judgment. Sinners will have no place among the godly." The ungodly, those who don't have a relationship with Christ and who don't follow the Word of God, will not have a place in heaven among those who do know the Lord. Instead, they will face an eternity separated from God.

But those who follow the Lord will live in heaven with Him forever. What is the condition of your soul today? Are you a Christ-follower? Is your relationship with Him growing stronger each day, and are you allowing Him to speak to you and mold you into the man or woman He intends you to be? Or are you like chaff in the wind, easily swayed from one belief to the next?

There is a life that is abundant and free and full of joy. It is the life that has learned to enjoy the fruits of godliness. The life of worship truly is a life worth living.

My trust is in You for salvation, Lord Jesus. I want to enjoy You forever in Your eternal home!

Worship Him as Mighty God

O LORD God of Heaven's Armies! Where is there anyone as mighty as you, O LORD? You are entirely faithful.

PSALM 89:8

He will be called: Wonderful Counselor, Mighty God" (Isaiah 9:6). Yes, Jesus is God. Colossians 1 and many other Scriptures attest to the fact that Jesus is not only the Savior of the world, but the Creator of the world, as well. He is God incarnate: God in the flesh.

The prophet Isaiah had clearly established this truth in his heart and mind. He didn't say, "He shall be Mighty God," as if by His resurrection He now suddenly had the right to become God. No, he said, "He shall be called Mighty God," both now and forever. He is mighty because He is all-powerful. He displayed part of His power through miracles in His ministry, but upon His resurrection, He conquered death itself.

He is mighty because He is the bridge between our lostness and salvation. There is no one and nothing else that can save us from our sin. Jesus is the only Way—the mediator between death and life eternal. And He is mighty because of His grace. His grace is broad enough to forgive every sin and sufficient to keep us held in His hands forever. Worship Jesus, the Mighty God.

Mighty God, I give You my praise and adoration!

Worship from His Word

How can a young person stay pure? By obeying your word. . . . I have hidden your word in my heart, that I might not sin against you.

PSALM 119:9, 11

I've referred to it before, but I love Psalm 1 because it gives us a very clear picture of how we can live either a victorious Christian life or a miserable one. The choice is up to us.

The first part of the psalm shows us the progression of walking into sin, standing in the midst of it, and eventually settling into that lifestyle. This doesn't mean that we shouldn't get to know the sinful and the rebellious. In fact, we should make it a point to reach out to them, as most of us were in that crowd at some point before Jesus saved us. Rather, this passage means that we should not adopt the practices and the lifestyle of the sinful, because it is destructive to our lives and the antithesis of godliness.

The second part of the chapter tells us that if we commit to the study of God's Word, our lives will be blessed and prosperous. As a tree gets its nutrients from the fertile soil, we get our spiritual nutrients from the Bible.

So the choice is up to us: Get our influence from the wrong source or the right Source. Worshipers always choose the right Source.

I choose You, Lord Jesus, the right Source. Help me turn my back on sin and immerse myself in Your Word.

Are You in Need of Some Peace and Quiet?

Fix your thoughts on what is true, and honorable, and right, and pure, and lovely, and admirable. Think about things that are excellent and worthy of praise.

PHILIPPIANS 4:8

The Bible tells us that the peace of God passes all understanding (Philippians 4:7). The word *understanding* used here is a direct reference to your thoughts. In other words, if you want the perfect peace of God in your life, it begins with your thought life.

Philippians 4:8 is a powerful verse. It is in this verse that Paul tells us to think on things that are true, noble, just, pure, lovely, and of good report. He encourages us to fix our minds on things that are worthy of praise and to consider deeply the words of wisdom we have been taught in Scripture, and then put them into practice. It is then that Paul says we will experience the peace of God.

Do you want some peace in your day? Then practice what you think. Put your thoughts into action by doing something for someone that is lovely, pure, and noble.

I could use some peace in my day, Lord! With Your help I fill my mind with things that are true, noble, just, pure, lovely, and of good report. Now, what can I do to bless someone today?

New Wine in New Skins

Anyone who belongs to Christ has become a new person. The old life is gone; a new life has begun!

2 CORINTHIANS 5:17

Have you ever wondered what Jesus meant when He said, "No one puts . . . new wine into old wineskins, or else the wineskins break, the wine is spilled and the wineskins are ruined. But they put new wine into new wineskins, and both are preserved" (Matthew 9:16–17 NKJV)? In this metaphor, the wine is the Holy Spirit and the wineskins are believers. If you put new, unfermented wine into an old wineskin, the fermentation process will eventually form gases that burst the old skin, destroying both the wine and the skin.

This is a picture of our salvation. When we receive salvation from God, we don't receive an improvement of our old nature. We don't just become a better person; we become a new person, like new wine going into new skin. Our very nature is completely transformed by the grace of God. The Lord tells us in Ezekiel, "I will give you a new heart, and I will put a new spirit in you. I will take out your stony, stubborn heart and give you a tender, responsive heart" (36:26).

That should give you plenty of reason to worship today!

Amen, Lord! Thank You for transforming me. The old has gone; the new has come!

Worship Like an Oak Tree

Blessed is the one who trusts in the LORD, whose confidence is in him. They will be like a tree planted by the water that sends out its roots by the stream. It does not fear when heat comes; its leaves are always green. It has no worries in a year of drought and never fails to bear fruit.

JEREMIAH 17:7–8 NIV

A few months ago, I was walking a golf course shooting my normal pitiful score, when on the eighth hole I came across one of the most beautiful oak trees I've ever seen. It was late fall, and many of its leaves had fallen off. My golf ball was lying at the base of that old tree. So in searching for my ball among the leaves, I noticed that it wasn't just leaves from the oak that I was kicking around, but also small leaves and chaff from other plants and trees along the fairway. The chaff is the light, insignificant stuff that blows so easily in the wind. When a gust comes, that's what moves first.

And so it is with those who aren't grounded in the Word of God. They are like the chaff in the wind, Psalm 1:4 says. They are easily blown about by the changing winds of cultural preference and shifting values. I encourage you today to be like that oak tree instead: steady and strong, trusting and worshiping our unshakable and unchangeable God.

Make me strong and steady and immovable like an oak tree, heavenly Father!

Immediately, Eventually, Ultimately

In my distress I cried out to the LORD; yes, I prayed to my God for help. He heard me from his sanctuary; my cry to him reached his ears.

PSALM 18:6

Do you spend enough time praying to Jesus? I know it's a simple question, but it's also a searching one. Prayer is hard. It takes an enormous amount of discipline and time. And sometimes we feel as though the Lord isn't hearing us, and even more frustrating, that He isn't answering us. But we can rest assured today that God does hear the prayers of His children, and He does answer them. His answers may not come in the form we wanted, or in the time we wanted, but He answers in one of three ways: immediately, eventually, or ultimately.

Prayer is the secret to a transformed life. The surrendered Christian life is impossible to live without constant, meaningful fellowship with the One who rescued your soul. Prayer allows you time to get to know Him better, to become familiar with His voice and His direction for your life.

So exercise faith in God today by trusting Him with your prayers. Then praise Him and worship Him in advance for answering those prayers. Talk to God, then listen to what He has to say to you.

Lord, there's so much room for improvement in my prayer life. Please help me!

Finishing Well

I focus on this one thing: Forgetting the past and looking forward to what lies ahead, I press on to reach the end of the race and receive the heavenly prize for which God, through Christ Jesus, is calling us.

PHILIPPIANS 3:13–14

I once recorded a song called "Finish Strong." The words go like this: "I want to finish strong, faithful to the finish though the road is long, crossing that line; and still I'm pressing on." These lyrics were inspired by the words of Paul: "I press toward the goal for the prize of the upward call of God in Christ Jesus" (Philippians 3:14 NKJV). Paul was not a quitter, and neither should we be. That's one of the cardinal rules in my household. We don't quit. We may lose, get hurt, get outplayed, but no quitting is allowed. We finish, and if at all possible, we finish strong.

There are countless stories in Scripture and throughout history of people of character who didn't quit, even when the odds were stacked against them. They pressed on. And as believers, even when it seems our friends, the culture, even the government is turning against us, we must keep pressing on, living for Him and loving those who don't know Him. Do it fearlessly, do it boldly, and do it passionately.

Live with nothing to prove, live with nothing to hide, live with nothing to lose. Jesus is worth it!

By Your grace, Lord Jesus, I will finish strong and never give up!

Worship the One and Only Jesus

He is the image of the invisible God, the firstborn over all creation. . . . All things were created through Him and for Him. And He is before all things, and in Him all things consist. And He is the head of the body, the church . . . that in all things He may have the preeminence.

COLOSSIANS 1:15–18 NKJV

Before the dawn of time, Jesus was there. He was there when the Father slung the stars into space and lit the sun with just a spoken word. He was there when God breathed life into Adam, delivered His people through Moses, and rescued them again through Joseph.

Jesus was there to give boldness to Jeremiah, strength to Samson, and protection to Ezra. And then, Jesus was walking among us. Fully God and fully man, on a mission to seek and to save those who were lost, He endured the cross. But three days later, He rose again. And now He is here. Always has been. Always will be. He was, is, and will for eternity be the Son of God and the Savior of the world.

His name is above every name. His place is above every place. His position is above every position. All things were created for Him, through Him, and to Him. He is the only one worthy of our praise. Worship Him today, and let His majesty consume your lifestyle of worship!

I worship You with all my heart today, Lord Jesus! You are worthy of all praise and glory!

You will be a good servant of Christ Jesus,
constantly nourished on the words of the faith
and of the sound doctrine
which you have been following.

1 TIMOTHY 4:6 NASB

ABOUT THE AUTHOR

CHARLES BILLINGSLEY is one of Christian music's most captivating inspirational voices. The singer, husband, father, and teacher is also a gifted writer and serves as worship leader for David Jeremiah events. When he is not appearing at concerts and conferences around the world, he is the worship pastor at Thomas Road Baptist Church and an artist-in-residence and instructor at Liberty University.

**IF YOU ENJOYED THIS BOOK, WILL YOU CONSIDER
SHARING THE MESSAGE WITH OTHERS?**

Mention the book in a blog post or through Facebook, Twitter, Pinterest, or upload a picture through Instagram.

Recommend this book to those in your small group, book club, workplace, and classes.

Head over to facebook.com/worthypublishing, "LIKE" the page, and post a comment as to what you enjoyed the most.

Tweet "I recommend reading #WordsOnWorship by @CBillingsley // @worthypub"

Pick up a copy for someone you know who would be challenged and encouraged by this message.

Write a book review online.

Visit us at worthypublishing.com

twitter.com/worthypub

worthypub.tumblr.com

facebook.com/worthypublishing

pinterest.com/worthypub

instagram.com/worthypub

youtube.com/worthypublishing